With the 'Old & Bold'
1795 to 1818

Charles Steevens

With the 'Old & Bold' 1795 to 1818

The reminiscences of an officer of H.M. 20th Regiment during the Napoleonic Wars

Charles Steevens

LEONAUR

With the 'Old & Bold'
1795 to 1818
*The reminiscences of an officer of
H.M. 20th Regiment during the
Napoleonic Wars*
by Charles Steevens

First published under the title
Reminiscences of My Military Life From 1795 to 1818

Leonaur is an imprint
of Oakpast Ltd

ISBN: 978-0-85706-164-5(hardcover)
ISBN: 978-0-85706-163-8 (softcover)

http://www.leonaur.com

Contents

Preface

The following *Reminiscences* were written, by my Father, many years after the occurrence of the incidents therein described; they must therefore be regarded as merely jottings—from memory—of the various and eventful scenes, in which the writer participated.

                                                    Nathl. Steevens.

London, February, 1878.

THE WRITER

OF THESE *REMINISCENCES*

DIED AT

CHELTENHAM, MARCH 9, 1861.

Generous as brave, Affection, kindness, were to him as needful as his daily bread.—Rogers

CHAPTER 1

I Join the 20th Regiment

I entered the Army the 30th of December, 1795, having been gazetted an ensign by purchase in His Majesty s *20th* Regiment, (whilst at Dr. Barrow's Academy in Soho Square, London), Lieut.-General West-Hyde being the colonel. I was at this time in my nineteenth year, having been born at Billericay, Essex, January 15th, 1777.

The regiment was at that time in the West Indies, but in the spring following (1796) they returned to England a complete skeleton, and I joined them at Exeter in the month of March. The present (1839) Sir Charles Des Vœux[1] joined the regiment with me, being an ensign in the *20th*; he was an old school-fellow of mine. We were quartered at Exeter until the autumn of 1796, when we were ordered to Lichfield. The Regiment at this time was commanded by Lieut.-Colonel Forbes Champagne, uncle to Sir Charles Des Vœux.

During our stay here two of our officers[2] went to the top of the Cathedral spire (by ladder) out of a freak; rather a mad one certainly, it being attended with danger.

We remained at Lichfield only a short time, and about March, 1797, we marched to Liverpool, at which time I was made Lieutenant without purchase. We remained here till the summer of 1798, and then we received a route for Manchester. About this time I was sent on the recruiting service to Ashton-under-Lyne, Lancashire.[3] I was

---

1. Sir Charles Des Vœux quitted the Regiment in 1800, having lost a leg in the action of the 10th September, 1799, near Crabbendam, in Holland.

2. One, I believe the present (1839) Major-General Wardlaw.

3. Where my second son, George Steevens, an Ensign in my old Regiment the *20th*, is now (July, 1839) quartered. He served in the *20th* Regiment from 1888 to 1857 when he retired (a Lieut.-Colonel) on half-pay: he died in February, 1857.

there a few weeks, and from thence I was sent to Bury, in the same county.

I cannot forbear mentioning a circumstance that took place while I was recruiting at Bury; though it may appear of little consequence, it was not so to *me*. I had been in Bury about three weeks, without anyone to speak to, except the man and his wife where I lodged, who were very civil to me.

Just picture to yourself a young recruiting-officer, in a small dull country town, wandering about, without any society, although daily meeting many gentlemen of the place at the reading room, only to be gazed at, (for at this time recruiting-officers always wore their uniform,) and, perhaps, by some looked upon as a scamp; for, by-the-by, the reason why I met with no civility was owing to the misconduct of the officer I relieved on the recruiting service; however, as good luck would have it, one fine morning the clergyman of the parish, who lived opposite to my lodgings and was a family man, called upon me and asked me to dine with him, an invitation I most readily and cheerfully accepted. I was there introduced to several other families, and passed a most agreeable time, till I was ordered to Derby on the same service, and I left Bury with much regret, as I had, met there with the greatest attention.

After I had left Bury some years, I heard, by accident, why the clergyman (the Rev. Mr. H-rgr—s) had called upon me; no doubt he must have repeatedly seen me going in and out of my lodgings, (his door being opposite to mine,) and I daresay fancied I must have a dull time of it, being always alone, and had therefore compassion on me; but it appears the reason why he called upon me was in consequence of a dream he had, *having dreamt I was a gentleman* the night before he called—and I hope his dream was verified; at any rate it was a pleasant dream for me, and I shall ever feel indebted to the Rev. Mr. H-rgr—s and his family for their kindness. From Bury I went to Derby, where I was for six months, until the summer of 1799, when I was ordered to Windsor to receive volunteers, for the *20th* Regiment, from the old Stafford Militia.

The regiment remained but a short time at Manchester, and from thence they went to Preston in the same county, and continued at Preston till they were ordered on the expedition to Holland, about

August, 1799; having previously received about 1800 volunteers from the different regiments of Militia, which gave us two battalions. The troops assembled at Barham Downs, in Kent, a short time before our embarkation, which took place at Deal, I think in the month of August.

Chapter 2

The Flander's Campaign

The *20th* Regiment were in General Don's[1] Division, and brigaded with the 63rd Regiment. We landed at the Helder, and our Division joined the Army, which had landed there a short time before under Sir Ralph Abercrombie, as ours was the second embarkation. I forgot to mention that at the time of our embarkation at Deal, the Division consisted of about 4,000 men, and everything was so well arranged, the boats being all ready for us on our arrival on the beach, that, from the time the Division stepped into the boats, it took only twenty minutes before all were on board, and it was telegraphed to the Admiralty.

On my first arrival in Holland I was quartered at the Texel Island, near the mouth of the Scheldt, where the Dutch Fleet lay, previous to their surrender to our Navy. We had 100 men on the island, commanded by Captain George Paddon of my regiment, and Lieutenant Robinson and I were the two subalterns of the detachment. I had often heard of barbers being surgeons, and such was the case in the Island of Texel; for the same person who attended our sick was the barber of the place, and he lived just outside the fort where we were quartered. At night we used to raise our drawbridge, and had it all snug to ourselves. We remained in the island about three weeks, and then joined "The Old and Bold" (as the *20th* was called) much to our joy, for we did not like being away, in case any action should take place during our absence. We had been daily on the look out to receive orders to join our regiment, and at last the welcome news arrived.

The two battalions of the *20th* Regiment were warmly engaged

---

1. General Don died many years after, Lieut.-Governor of Gibraltar.

with the enemy on the 10th September at Crabbendam. The enemy consisted of French and Dutch troops, for many Dutch opposed us. Our two battalions suffered very much in this action, and we had several officers very severely wounded, and two of them lost a leg each.[2] The *20th* Regiment were highly complimented by Sir Ralph Abercrombie for their conduct in the above action. The following was in Orders:—

> The two battalions of the *20th* Regiment, posted opposite to Crabbendam and Zypher-Sluys, did credit to the high reputation which that regiment has always borne. Lieut-Colonel Smyth of that corps, who had the particular charge of that post, received a severe wound in his leg, which will deprive us for a time of his services.

In this action Lieut.-Colonel Smyth commanded the First Battalion and Lieut.-Colonel Clephane[3] the Second Battalion of the *20th*.

The regiment was afterwards engaged in the action of the 2nd October, and had two officers wounded;[4] and they were very warmly engaged on the 6th October near Egmont-op-Zee, in which action they had two officers killed, and eight wounded in the two battalions.[5]

---

2. Soon after the battle of Crabbendam Sir Ralph Abercrombie was superseded in his command by the Duke of York. 1st Battalion *20th* Regiment.—*Wounded,*—Lieut.-Colonel Smyth, severely; afterwards Sir George Smyth, and died Major-General, an excellent officer. Major Robert Ross, afterwards Major-General, and killed at Baltimore, 1814.—*Vide* Appendix A. Captain Henry Powlett.
Lieutenant John Colborne, afterwards Field-Marshal Lord Seaton. Lieutenant Charles Des Vœux, lost a leg; now (1839) Sir Charles Des Vœux, Bart.
Lieutenant Christopher Hamilton, lost a leg; now (1839) Major-General, commanded 97th Regiment for many years. Lieutenant and Adjutant Samuel South, afterwards (1818) rose to command the *20th* Regiment. 2nd Battalion.—*Wounded.*—Captain-Lieutenant L. Ferdinand Adams.
3. Lieut.-Colonel Clephane died many years after a Major-General, having for some time been an M.P.
4. Captain Powlett 1st Battalion), and Ensign Mills (2nd Battalion).
5. 1st Battalion.—*Killed.*—Brevet Lieut.-Colonel Philip Bainbrigge, commanding 1st Battalion *20th* Regiment, and Ensign Mc Currie.—*Wounded,*—Brevet-Major Campbell, died of his wounds. Captain Newman; killed in a duel at Malta, in 1802, by Lieut.-Colonel B—— who was dismissed the service in consequence. Lieutenant Steevens, severely; taken prisoner. Ensign Favell, severely; taken prisoner and died of his wounds at Amsterdam.
2nd. Battalion.—*Wounded.*—Captain Maister, severely; afterwards Major-General. Captain Wallace; died of wounds received in the Pyrenees, 25th July, 1813. Captain Torrens, severely. Ensign Drewry.

I was amongst the number, being very severely wounded, and afterwards taken prisoner by the French cavalry at Egmont-op-Zee on the morning of the 8th; our Army having commenced their retreat on the evening of the 7th, leaving their own wounded behind, as well as the wounded prisoners.[6]

I was Lieutenant of grenadiers at the time I was wounded, but had command of a battalion company; and Ensign Favell and myself, who were the only officers of that company, were both wounded before a single man of the company were hit, which was a proof that we were picked off by the French riflemen, numbers of which they had in front of their Army; we, unfortunately, had but few in front of ours, and they, I believe, belonged to the 60th Rifles. The riflemen the enemy had gave them a great advantage over us, and in consequence of their having so many light troops many of our officers were picked off by them, and the proportion of killed and wounded officers was very great; but we are wiser now, and can show as good a front as the enemy whenever we have an opportunity to cope with them.[7]

I fortunately was carried off the field by a private of the 15th Light Dragoons.[8] I was placed on his horse in front of him, seated sideways, with a blanket thrown round me, and a man led the horse, as he was very high spirited, and I could not bear him to go beyond a foot's pace; for my wound being in the leg I suffered much pain from the position in which I was placed. I recollect offering the dragoon some money, but he refused to take anything on my arrival at the town of Egmont-op-Zee. I was there placed in a house upon a bed of hay, on the floor, with other wounded officers of my own regiment, where I was taken prisoner on the 8th.

The wounded of course passed an anxious night on the 7th, expecting the enemy to enter the town every moment. As soon as daylight appeared in galloped the French cavalry, sword in hand. One

6. Lieut.-Colonel Bainbrigge and Major Campbell were buried at Egmont-op-Zee; the latter by the French, as he died of his wounds after the English retired from that place.

7. The marked difference between the uniforms of the officers and privates at that time also accounted for so many of the former being easily distinguished and picked off.

8. I fell in with him once or twice in England afterwards, as I always found him out whenever I happened to be quartered in the same place with the 15th Dragoons, feeling very grateful for the care he took of me.

came into the room where I was lying, attended by my servant, Private Thomas Lamb, who was taken prisoner with me, as, when I was left behind at Egmont-op-Zee, he would not leave me, but was determined to share my fate. Immediately the Frenchman saw me he said "*Qui êtes vous*"?

I answered "*Un officier Anglais*"; he then said "*Les officiers sont braves, mais les soldats ne le sont pas,*" and taking up my canteen drank part of its contents, which consisted of either white brandy or hollands; he then left the room; others came in, amongst whom was a French officer; I was glad to see him, as I expected to be well used, and I found it to be the case, for the French officers treated us prisoners with the greatest humanity and attention.

Soon after the French entered Egmont-op-Zee preparations were made to remove the wounded out of the town towards the rear. Poor Favell and I were put into the same open Dutch wagon, and were taken that night to Alkmaar, where we were put into a hospital for the night. Here our wounds were dressed (I mean Favell's and mine, for my servant was not wounded). There were a great many Dutch females in the hospital, making bandages and assisting the wounded; some appeared to be ladies, for there were Dutch officers and men, as well as French and English, in the hospital. The French General (Le Brun) promised that my servant should remain with me, but it was not attended to, and poor Tom Lamb was put into prison with the other soldiers who were taken, and I heard nothing of him for many months.

We were about a week or ten days reaching Breda; we were laid generally in our clothes upon mattresses, sometimes being carried into an inn. We suffered much from the jolting of the wagons, and at one time we were obliged to halt for a day or so to recruit our strength, for it was very fatiguing travelling so many days in open wagons, without our clothes being taken off, and the surgeons were fearful and apprehensive lest some of us should be thrown into a fever. The journey to Breda was very harassing, the wounded being conveyed in boats by canal, as well as in wagons; but being at that time a young man (not twenty-three years of age) I was able to undergo the hardships and fatigue to which we were exposed.

Whenever we arrived at a town in the evening where we were to halt for the night, I, being unable to walk, was carried by the French soldiers and placed upon a mattress, either in an inn or hospital, and the next morning carried out again and replaced in a boat or wagon, just as it happened. One day the French soldiers were carrying me through the streets with other wounded English officers, and a party of Dutch insulted us by hooting, etc. The French soldiers immediately drove them off with the butt-end of their muskets, and no doubt would have floored a few of them if they had not made themselves scarce. The French always behaved well to us, but the Dutch were very boorish and uncivil

Previous to our arrival at Breda I parted with poor Favell; he was dangerously wounded in the breast, and although we travelled together for several days he never spoke; he was left at Amsterdam, where, I believe, he died, poor fellow; I was many years afterwards acquainted with his brother in the 61st Regiment.

On our arrival at Breda I was put into a very large hospital with some other English officers; it was one of the *Stadtholder's* palaces converted into a hospital. Here also were numerous French and Dutch officers and many hundreds of wounded soldiers. I was very kindly treated during the time I remained in the hospital both by the surgeons and physicians who attended the wounded and sick, as also by the French officers who were in the same room with me. Our party consisted of about eight, three of which were of our army, *viz*. Captain John McLean,[9] 92nd Regiment, an officer of the 35th Regiment of the name of Nichols, and myself. Lieut. Nichols, poor fellow, died very suddenly; he rose from his bed and limped to my bedside, and sitting down had a long chat with me, for at that time I could not get up; he had not returned to his bed more than an hour, when a violent haemorrhage took place and he died, poor fellow, in a few minutes. I was much shocked, and hardly closed my eyes that night, his death was so sudden and unexpected. He appeared a nice gentlemanly young fellow, and, had his life been spared, no doubt we should have been intimate friends. I believe his father was a barrister.

To point out how very attentive and polite the French officers were, who were lying wounded in the same room where I was in the Breda Hospital, they never partook of anything, when our meals

9. Now (1839) Sir John McLean, and a major-general.

16

were brought in, until we three prisoners were helped to whatever we preferred; and the French officers never came into the room, where we were all lying in our beds, without either taking off or touching their caps, as a salute, and saying, "*Bon jour*," or on retiring, "*Bon soir, citoyens*," the term of address always made use of during the reign of Napoleon.

Another instance of their attention to the British officers took place as they were conducting us through the country, for they never would allow the Russian officers (also prisoners of war) to be put into the same room with us, whenever we halted in any town, but put them in a room by themselves. One day, whilst in Breda Hospital, I recollect the French officers were very much offended at a host of English officers, (who by some unforeseen accident had been taken prisoners in one of the actions), coming into the room to see us without doffing or touching their cocked hats; it just shews to what extremes the French frequently carry their *politesse*.

One of the officers who came to visit us happened to be named Petit; he was a major in the 35th Regiment, and, being a stout, fat-looking man they used often to joke about his name being "Petit"; and he being one of the number who had hurt their feelings by transgressing, as they supposed, the laws of politeness, his name was often called in question.

Another instance of their good feeling towards us prisoners of war occurred after the death of Lieutenant Nichols. Previous to his interment, some of the officers of his regiment (the 35th) expressed a wish to have the coffin opened, and they discovered that every article of apparel had been taken off the body; it was reported to the superintendent of the hospital, and it was ascertained that the man who attended our room, where Lieut. Nichols died, had committed the robbery; the French authorities insisted upon his dismissal, and he would have lost his situation had we not all interceded on his behalf; but as he was particularly attentive to us wounded during our sufferings we begged him off, and he continued in the hospital. I was several weeks in this hospital, and then we were all allowed to return to England on our parole; we were conveyed to the Helder sometimes in carriages or wagons, and occasionally by canal or river: I recollect crossing two branches of the Rhine, the Waal and the Maas.

CHAPTER 3

Back to England

Fortunately for me, on our arrival at the Helder, I fell in with two companies of my own regiment commanded by Captain Weldon;[1] they were embarked on board a gun-brig, and happy I was to join them. We had a quick passage, and put into Yarmouth; the companies disembarked here, and then marched to Norwich, where the *20th* regiment was quartered. We were in some danger as we approached Yarmouth, it being a dark night, about the end of November, and we hardly knew where we were; after having passed two or three buoys, being in soundings, it was thought best to let go the anchor, for there was a consultation on the subject, and charts and maps were brought into the cabin to endeavour to find out where we were by the colour of the buoys, which were sometimes white and sometimes not; it was blowing fresh, and, unfortunately, the officer who commanded the gun-brig, was in that state when he did not know the head from the stern, and not any one on board seemed to like taking the responsibility on himself.

At last the *lieutenants lady*, who happened to be on board, gave the word, "Let go the anchor," and it was immediately "let go"; and in the morning, at daylight, we found ourselves close off Yarmouth. This may appear an odd story, but I can vouch for the authenticity of it, for I was lying in my cot in the cabin, still suffering from my wound, and heard and saw all that was going on, and glad enough we all were when safe at anchor.

After I landed at Yarmouth, Lieutenants Russell, Robinson, and I got into a cart and proceeded to Norwich to join our regiment.

1. He died in Sicily, 1806.

At that time, being a prisoner of war, I could not remain to do duty with the *20th*; besides, I was still very lame, my wound not having yet healed; I therefore had leave of absence, and went to London and remained there till I had so far recovered as to be able to walk about. I was staying at Mr. Orlton's house in Blackfriar's Road for some weeks, his son being an old friend of mine, now, poor fellow, deceased. At this time (January, 1800) I was made captain in the *20th* by purchase.

The *20th* Regiment soon after marched to Ashford, in Kent, where they were quartered a few months, and were then ordered to Ireland in the summer of 1800; here they were quartered in Cork, and from thence they embarked for Belle-Isle, a small island on the coast of France, not far from Finisterre; after being there a short time they sailed for the Mediterranean, and ultimately went to the island of Minorca.

About the month of March (1800) I was exchanged for a Dutch officer, having been a few months in England on my parole; I was then with the *20th* at Ashford, and was ordered thence to Canterbury to take charge of a detachment of the regiment, consisting of men who had returned from Holland, where they had been prisoners of war.

The 4th of June, the same year, the detachment commenced their march to Liverpool, having, a few days previously, received a route to proceed there. Our party consisted of about 150 men and several officers, for the men of the 2nd Battalion had just joined us. When we arrived at Lichfield we found a route at the Post Office ordering us to Hilsea Barracks, near Portsmouth, instead of Liverpool; we halted a week at Lichfield, and then started for Hilsea. After about six weeks march from the time we left Canterbury we reached the barracks, a few miles from Portsmouth. What a circuitous route! if we had been ordered to Deal to embark for Minorca—one day's march instead of six weeks'—what an expense Government might have been saved; but things are managed differently now-a-days. I was very glad indeed to see again my servant (Lamb), who joined us here, having been exchanged; such a figure as he was, poor fellow, having hardly a rag to his back, for the French had robbed him of every article but the clothes he had on.[2]

---

2. He continued my servant for several years afterwards, and was a very faithful, honest fellow; he served some years as a non-commissioned officer, and was discharged, a sergeant, in 1818; I was sorry to hear that he was some time afterwards confined as a lunatic in Lancaster Castle.

While at Hilsea we were daily expecting to be ordered to embark for the Mediterranean to join the regiment, which was at Minorca, or on its way to that island; at length, after having been about three months at Hilsea, we embarked at Spithead, (I think in the month of October) on board the *Harmony*, Transport No. 48.

On the 6th of November, 1800, while we lay at Spithead, we had a most violent gale of wind, a complete hurricane; we had three anchors down, and yet drifted; but at last the ship brought up, and we held on by our anchors. Captain Rose (*20th*) and I were lying on the locker looking out of the cabin window during the gale, the vessel pitching most tremendously, when she was struck at the stern and shipped a sea which sent Rose and myself headlong on the cabin floor, but we were young at this time and laughed it off.

The master's name was Captain Wilson, a most excellent sailor; he seldom or ever quitted the deck, either night or day, in bad weather, and we had a pretty good share of it; Wilson was a most civil and kind-hearted man, and made our situation in his ship as comfortable to all of us as he possibly could. Our medical officer was Mr. Howship,[3] hospital mate, who was very attentive to the few sick that were on board.

During the hurricane, which we encountered at Spithead, on the 6th November, hardly a man-of-war could hold by her anchors; it was so violent at one time that even the *Royal William* (the *Royal Billy*, as the sailors called her), drifted from her moorings, and several ships were stranded; but Providence was kind to us and we rode it out in safety. The gale lasted about six hours, from 10 a.m. to 4 p.m., and it was afterwards a calm evening. During the storm, ships were constantly drifting past us, and also pieces of wreck, parts of masts, spars, rigging, etc. In our vessel we were obliged to have men standing by the windlass, to throw buckets of water over it, as it frequently took fire by the friction of the cable. We sailed once or twice from Spithead, but were always driven back by contrary winds; we sailed for the last time about the middle of December (1800), but the return of foul winds obliged us to put into Falmouth.

It was a fine sight to see the convoy when in the Channel, for our

3. Mr. Howship is now (1839) a surgeon in great practice, at 21, Savile Row, London, and Surgeon of Charing Cross Hospital: my eldest son, Charles, was a pupil of his for several years, having studied for the medical profession.

fleet (the Mediterranean) having been joined by the West India fleet, we both consisted of about 500 sail, and the weather was very pleasant between Spithead and Falmouth. It being very difficult to get a large convoy out of that harbour without a leading wind, we were therefore detained five weeks at Falmouth.

During the time we were there, several of us used to go out shooting, and although we were embarked in a small transport, and could not make any great display of plate at our table, we had a good supply of game, frequently hares, snipe, partridges, etc., hanging over the stern; but latterly our supply was completely cut off, for one day I was out shooting with a brother officer. Captain Alexander Rose; we had but one gun, and that belonged to me; I had lent him the gun to take a shot or two, and a dog happening to come across our path. Rose let fly at him, and slightly hit the animal; he then gave me the gun. The farmers came out, hearing the dog yelping, and made towards us; my brother sportsman ran off, and I, being in possession of the gun, though perfectly innocent of having fired at the dog, was obliged to take to my heels, otherwise no doubt I should have come in for a little of the "condign," as most likely they would not have believed my story; so that, after this foolish frolic, we went no more on shore shooting; instead of our having game, it appears game had been made of us; and in lieu of those luxuries we had plenty of salt junk.

We did not leave Falmouth until the end of January, 1801, the convoy being accompanied by the *Sea Horse* frigate, Captain Foote, and I think, the *Maidstone* frigate,

During our voyage to Lisbon we had dreadfully stormy weather, and a very boisterous passage across the Bay of Biscay; one day we encountered a most tremendous heavy, rolling sea, without any wind, in the Bay; such a sea as I never before, nor since, witnessed; it came rolling towards us like mountain after mountain. There were many ships in the convoy, and when we happened to be in the trough of the sea we could not even discern the top-gallant-mast head of any of the other ships; but when we happened to be on the top of one of these mountainous waves, the fleet was then visible. I never could have supposed it possible for a ship to live in such a sea, for when a wave approached us it appeared to be far above our top-gallant-mast head, and seemed as though it would overwhelm us; but as the wave

21

neared us, our little transport rode up it in a most wonderful manner. Our rigging was very much strained, and Wilson, our excellent commander, was fearful we should carry away our masts; but through the aid of Divine Providence we got through it all safe.

During our gale we had to lay-to a whole day and part of a night; at last Wilson, and several others who had the command of transports, being apprehensive that we were approaching a lee shore, made sail without waiting for orders from the commodore, and stole away in the night, and we fortunately soon reached the Tagus. We then found there were some of our convoy missing, which were discovered to have been lost on the Berlins—some rocks off the coast of Portugal—and in one of the transports lost were several officers of the 17th Regiment with whom I was acquainted, for we had often met ashore at Falmouth.

CHAPTER 4

To Minorca

We remained at Lisbon about a week to repair damages and to have our rigging put in order, under the superintendence of our indefatigable captain. I often thought that if he had not been a very skilful and steady seaman our situation would frequently have been very precarious. All damages having been repaired, and our scattered convoy collected, we sailed for Minorca, which we reached in about three weeks. From the time we embarked at Portsmouth till the vessel reached Minorca, at the end of March, 1801, the troops had been on board six months; nevertheless they were very healthy, and I have always found soldiers very happy and contented at sea, which I attribute to their easy life, having little to do whilst embarked.

We found the old *20th* quartered in several parts of the island; the 1st Battalion were at George Town, and the 2nd Battalion at Fort George, a fort commanding the entrance of the harbour, which led to Port Mahon, a remarkably fine, sheltered harbour, where an immense fleet of men-of-war could ride in safety in any weather. Some of the *20th* were detached along the coast in the Martello towers; I was stationed at Fort George, having been promoted captain into the 2nd Battalion a short time back.

The following occurrence took place whilst our 2nd Battalion was quartered at Fort George:—There was a battery of two guns, of rather large calibre, a short distance from the fort, where there was a Captain's Guard, and his orders were not to allow any merchant ship, transport, or small ship, to come in or go out of the harbour without hailing them; and, with regard to men-of-war, whenever they sailed *at night,* the orders were that the officer of the guard, at the battery, should be apprised of it.

One night a large ship was going out, and the officer of the guard, Captain Edmund Byron, of the *20th* Regiment was placed in a rather awkward situation; he had not been made acquainted with her sailing, and as soon as she came within hail of the battery he ordered the bombardier to hail her, but no notice was taken of it; she was hailed a second time, and told if she did not answer or lay-to she would be fired at; still no reply; so the officer commanding the guard ordered the bombardier to prime the gun and to fire near her; the shot however passed between her fore and mainmast; she then immediately backed her main-topsail and sent an officer on shore. The ship turned out to be His Majesty's brig *Speedy*, commanded by Lord Cochrane,[1] and a most gallant officer his lordship was.

He was highly incensed that his ship should have been fired at, but the captain of the guard explained to the lieutenant who came ashore that he had acted agreeably to his orders; and on Lord Cochrane representing the affair to General Fox,[2] who commanded the troops at the time, no fault was found with Captain Byron, as it was impossible for him to know what ship was going out. It might have been one of the Danish men-of-war which had been captured, several of which were there; the officer of the guard ought, therefore, to have been apprised of the *Speedy* sailing; so the complaint made ended in smoke, although a shot had been fired.

If one of these captured men-of-war had escaped, Captain Byron, in all probability, would have stood a fair chance of losing his commission; his position as captain of that guard was therefore a responsible one.

Men-of-war, according to etiquette, never allow themselves to be hailed, but in this instance it was very properly broken through; ever afterwards the officer of the guard was always informed whenever a man-of-war sailed out of the harbour *at night*.

The guard house was beautifully situated, having a fine, commanding view of the harbour; I have often mounted guard there myself, and having a good telescope, I found it very valuable and amusing when on this duty.

---

1. Afterwards Earl Dundonald.
2. Brother to Charles James Fox, the celebrated statesman..

We did not find Minorca an unpleasant quarter, being able to ride a good deal about the island, and visit our friends at the outposts; for General Fox was extremely liberal in allowing forage to officers of *all* ranks, to enable them to keep horses; and when we left the island, those that were fit for the cavalry were purchased for a troop of dragoons which was raised in Minorca, seventy dollars being the price allowed; so I was pretty well remunerated for my young black long-tail; how very different to what it is nowadays, as the *commanding officer* of an infantry regiment is only allowed forage for one horse, though he may have been twenty years in command; and at the time I am now speaking of the *junior ensign* in Minorca had the allowance. What would Joe Hume, the clipper of wings, say to this?

At the time the *20th* were in the island the regiment was composed of limited service men, raised from the Militia and enlisted not to serve out of Europe; but, being very anxious to go to Egypt, the officers exerted themselves to get the men to volunteer, which they did most cheerfully and willingly, and each man received an additional bounty.

We soon after (some time about June, 1801,) embarked for Egypt; the idea of having an opportunity of meeting the enemy again made us all alive, and we left the island in great spirits, and as we went round Cape Mola we gave three hearty cheers.

CHAPTER 5

Egypt

Sir Ralph Abercrombie had landed in Egypt with an army on the 8th March, 1801, he was killed in the action of the 21st March, and General (afterwards Lord) Hutchinson succeeded to the command. We reached Aboukir Bay in about three weeks and soon after landed; we were encamped for sometime close to Pompey's Pillar, not far from Alexandria.

The 1st Battalion of the *20th* was engaged with the French one evening near that place, having attacked and driven in their pickets. We found the climate excessively hot, and being encamped on a sandy plain the heat in our tents was very oppressive; most of the officers for some time had nothing but the common bell tent, and many suffered considerably from fever, dysentery, and opthalmia; several of the *20th* officers were quite blind for a time, having the complaint in both eyes. Captain Arthur Lloyd suffered greatly from opthalmia, and some years afterwards lost his sight.[1]

Quartermaster Hoath[2] likewise lost an eye from the same cause. Several of the soldiers entirely lost their sight, and immense numbers were attacked by the complaint. It was a melancholy sight to see strings of soldiers leading each other to the hospital tent of a morning; some could see a little so as to be able to conduct those who, for a time, were quite deprived of sight.

Violent fever also attacked both officers and men, but did not prove fatal in many cases. Captain Byron and I were both very ill; and we lost

---

1. Now (1839) Major-General residing in Canada, and quite blind; he has a grant of land in that country, and has a most active wife, who superintends his affairs.
2. Now (1839) on half-pay.

one officer by fever, Lieut. Henry William Walker, a young man very much liked in the regiment. I entirely escaped the opthalmia.

Whilst we were in Egypt we made parties to go and visit the Pyramids. I went with a party of about six, and a pleasant time we had of it; I cannot recollect the names of all those who went with me, but Captain Byron, Lieut. Fulton, and, I think, Captain Murdoch McLean,[3] all of the *20th*, were among the number. We went from Alexandria in a large boat called a *Jerm*.

These boats were large and half-decked, and had one immense sail, with a crew of about a dozen sailors—Arabs—fine stout fellows. The Nile winding so much, the sail was at times of no use; the Arabs then took to the water, like so many large Newfoundland dogs, after taking off their dress, which consisted frequently of only a long blue cotton shirt, from the neck to the ankles.

After towing the boat round a winding part of the river, they plunged into the water some way ahead of the boat, and, as the *Jerm* approached them, they came alongside, climbed up the sides in all directions, and were very soon in their blue dresses again. These active fellows were in the water a dozen times or more a day, but never for any length of time, for the Nile was very rapid, and they never took to the water as long as the sail was of use.

We sailed up the Nile, touching at Rosetta and some other places on our way, where we used to supply ourselves with milk, eggs, fruit, bread, etc. We were two days before we reached Grand Cairo; here we fell in with another party, and amongst them was an officer of the 31st Regiment, Captain Blomer,[4] a very old friend and brother officer of mine, having served some years in the *20th* with me. We used to lodge together when quartered at Liverpool, in 1797 and 1798, and were particularly intimate friends; being both named Charles, we always called each other "Charley."

---

3. Killed at the battle of Maida, July 4, 1806.

4. My dear friend Captain Blomer was a great entomologist, and had a splendid collection of British insects, the collecting of which afforded him much amusement and occupation after he retired on half-pay, which he was obliged to do on account of ill-health, and, poor fellow, he died in the Isle of Wight, in May, 1836, in consequence of the breaking out of an old wound, leaving a widow, and one son who was studying for the law. I say a good deal about my kind friend and brother officer, not only on account of the affection I had for him, but also because his kindness and good temper were so well known to all my family.

Whilst in the neighbourhood of Cairo he shot a pelican, a nice little bird to fill a shooting jacket pocket. I saw it alive at Cairo, it being only winged; what became of it afterwards I forget.

The day after our arrival at Grand Cairo we visited the Pyramids. We went part of the way in a boat, as the Nile had overflowed some of the country between Cairo and the Pyramids; it was curious enough to be rowing over places which a short time previously had been perfectly dry, every now and then passing by trees half under water; but, as soon as the Nile subsided, the ground would, we were told, become as dry as before.

We visited the large Pyramid and went over the inside of it; there was a sarcophagus in the interior, which some called Pharoah's coffin; it was of dark granite and open. I saw nothing particularly-striking in the inside of the Pyramid, but altogether it was a most wonderful structure; such a quantity of large pieces of stone, so placed as to form high steps from the bottom to the top. I went part of the way, but had not nerve to reach the summit, neither had my friend Byron; I was much disappointed not being able to do so; but I never could bear to look down from a height, even when quite a boy; it was not therefore likely I should be able to reach the top of such a pyramid. Lieut. Fulton reached the top, and so did his servant, who was a fine tall fellow in our grenadier company; he was the only one who cleared the base by throwing a stone from the top of the Pyramid, as it required great strength of arm to throw that distance, and he was also the first at the summit, being a very active young man.

After quitting the Pyramid we took a look at the Sphinx, but so much of it was buried in the sand, that the head and face were only visible, and the latter was much defaced; if it were all uncovered no doubt it would be an enormous figure, as the head was very large; the face was not very handsome. When we had finished gazing at the Sphinx our party returned to Cairo, being all much gratified with our day's amusement.

We could get but little rest at night at Cairo on account of the mosquitoes, which tormented us dreadfully, and they were equally troublesome at Rosetta, on our way to and from Cairo, and I returned to camp very lame, having been severely bitten in the instep, for their bite seemed almost poisonous.

While we were at Rosetta we met one or two parties, and with one of them was an old brother officer, of the *20th*, Captain Colborne.[5] He was very much teased with the mosquitoes one night, when many of us were lying down to rest in a large room at one of the inns at Rosetta; he thought he would hit upon a plan to give the mosquitoes the slip, thinking they were on the walls of the room; he therefore shifted his bed to the middle of the room, and, much to our amusement, the mosquitoes attacked him worse than ever, and I believe few of us had any rest that night; we tried to smoke them out, but all would not do, and we arose in the morning very little refreshed.

On my return, after a very pleasant sail down the Nile, I found my regiment still in their encampment, where I left them, but we shortly after marched a little further into the country, where we again soon pitched our tents, and where we suffered dreadfully from want of water. We used to have watering parties commanded by officers, and had about four miles to go over the sandy plain, in very hot weather, and, after all, the water was brackish; being carried in the soldiers' canteens it was warm when It reached the camp, and a great deal of it was drunk on the way, which made our supply sometimes but scanty. The water was procured by digging large holes in the sand near the underground springs, and letting the water ooze into these hollows; and, after all our toil and trouble, it was hardly fit to drink, but we had no other water, it was therefore Hobson's choice. The want of wholesome water was unfortunately the cause of much sickness amongst us while we were in this encampment.

We were ordered early one morning to march to the Green Hill—why so called I cannot recollect, for there appeared no verdure on the place, as far as I can remember—it was not a great way from our camp; there were not many shots exchanged with the enemy that morning; the French fired a few cannon shot, which did but little execution, and I believe but few were put *hors de combat*. The 30th Regiment were engaged on this occasion; it was a short business, and we returned very soon again to our former encampment. Shortly after this the French

5. Now (1889) Lieut.-General Sir John Colborne, G.C.B. and G.C.H., Governor General, Civil and Military, in North America, and afterwards F. M. Lord Seaton, G.C.B., etc.

capitulated and left the country.

After we had been a few months in Egypt we embarked for the island of Malta, which part of the regiment reached in about three weeks, after a pleasant voyage; but one ship, the *Madras*, I think was her name, on board of which we had two companies, was nearly lost. It turned out that the ship sprung a leak, and the crew and troops on board were at the pumps for a fortnight; Sir Richard Bickerton, the Admiral, was on board; they came into Malta harbour with about seven feet of water in the hold.

The officers of the ship, as well as those of the troops embarked, took their turn at the pumps, and Sir Richard said, if there had not been troops on board she must have gone down, as numbers kept her afloat; the crew would have been exhausted by their fatigue and over-exertion, but having 150 soldiers on board it was a great relief to the sailors: happily Providence was bountiful, and they arrived in safety. The two companies of the *20th* were under the command of Captain Wallace;[6] Lieut. Edward Jackson[7] was also on board. The old *Madras*, I believe, never left Malta after this voyage.

The ship on board which I came from Egypt had a very quick passage; it blew one morning so hard (but it happened to be a fair wind) that the number of knots, which we ran in six hours, was, as stated in the log, one fourteen, three elevens, and two nines, which was good sailing, considering the vessel was an old forty-four gun ship and a bad sailer; Captain Preston commanded her, but I cannot recollect her name.

---

6. Afterwards Bt. Lieut.-Colonel.

7. Now (1839) Lieut.-Colonel Unattached, and a K.H.

CHAPTER 6

Malta & Leave

We disembarked shortly after our arrival at Malta, and were quartered at Isola; this was about November or December, 1801. The 1st Battalion were at Vittorioso, the opposite side of the harbour to us, commanded by Lieut.-Colonel George Smyth; the battalion to which I belonged was under the command of Lieut.-Colonel David Clephane. We remained in the island until 1805.

In 1802 I went on leave to England; on the way home we touched at Gibraltar, and stayed there a few days. My friend Captain Byron and I went over the "Rock," and visited the casemates and chambers, cut out in the rock for the cannon, which were very curious. It is a strong place, these chambers being one above another in rows, so that on the Spanish side of the "Rock" it is particularly strong, and there is a battery called the Devil's Tongue opposite the neutral ground facing the Spanish lines, which is a very formidable battery. We went to the top of the "Rock," where we saw a great many monkeys; the Governor did not allow them to be destroyed, so they were very numerous; you may always find them on the side of the "Rock" sheltered from the winds.

We were nearly meeting with an accident as we neared the "Rock," and were sailing round one of the points to the harbour. Our vessel being high out of the water, laden with hemp, and a good deal of sail set, a sudden gust of wind almost capsized us, and some of us were obliged to hold on, fearing we should have fallen overboard. The vessel was an old storeship, commanded by a master in the navy of the name of Price. The wind used to come on so unexpectedly, and in such frequent gusts, round the "Rock," that there was an order forbidding boats to carry sail in the harbour, as these sudden squalls were sometimes very violent and dangerous.

It was amusing to watch a curious kind of small sea-gull in the harbour that used to dive after the fish; it rose to some height then darted down, with its wings closed, with great force into the water, and appeared to go down some depth; the noise caused by this sudden dash into the water resembled throwing a sharp stone edgeways, with great force, into a deep stream.

After remaining a few days at Gibraltar we left for England. One night, while sailing before the wind with a fine summer breeze, the wind suddenly *chopped right round*; it was so unexpected, so sudden, and blew so strong, that they were obliged to cut away the haulyards to let the yards down upon the caps, fearing our top-gallant masts, or something worse, might have been carried away; however we fortunately received no damage: we afterwards had some foul winds, much to the annoyance of us landsmen, for I was always a bad sailor and not a very patient one.

After a pleasant passage of about three weeks we arrived at Plymouth; here the ship was put in quarantine for three or four days; the passengers then landed. My friend Byron stayed a week at Plymouth with me, and we then started for London to visit our friends. There were some officers of other regiments in the ship with us, and, on leaving Plymouth several of them proposed walking to London dressed as sailors, but told us (who posted it) not to notice them if we fell in with them on the road; however, as luck would have it, we saw them standing at an inn door as we drove up to change horses, I think it was at Cranford Bridge, and by our quizzing them their disguise was discovered; they accomplished their journey and were much amused with their frolic; we often met afterwards.

I went occasionally to see my relations at Billericay, in Essex, and after remaining in England until the summer following (1803), once more embarked to return to Malta to join my regiment; fifteen of us went out in the same ship, all of the *20th*, Colonel Robert Ross, Dr. Arnott our surgeon, Captain Byron, Captain Telford, Lieut. Dumas,[1] and several others whose names I cannot recollect; the name of the

---

1. Now (1839) Lieut.-Colonel, half-pay, and Deputy Governor of Tilbury Fort; after he left the *20th* he commanded the 2nd (or Queen's) in the West Indies.

transport was the *Queen*, and a most civil good seaman the master of her was. We embarked at Spithead, and were detained at the Isle of Wight by contrary winds; but at last we sailed rather suddenly.

A party of us were on shore at Ryde, and one fine summer morning about the month of August, between three and four o'clock, a signal gun was heard, which turned out to be from our commodore's ship for the fleet to get under weigh and immediately go to sea; a pretty rout it caused among us, scrambling out of bed and getting dressed to repair on board, which was accomplished in a very short time; the ship was under weigh when we got along side; having a fair wind we soon lost sight of the island, and ran down Channel in a very short time, and in a few days were far away from Old England. We were most of us young men and unmarried, and went to sea in very good spirits, looking forward at the end of our voyage, to meet again our brother officers at Malta. Mrs. Ross was with her husband (the colonel), and this was the commencement of her campaigning.

On our way out we touched at Gibraltar, which was my second visit to the "Rock," and while there many of us used to bathe from our ship in the harbour by jumping overboard, for we could swim very well, and the weather being excessively hot made us enjoy a plunge. One morning my old friend Dr. Archibald Arnott and I actually plunged into the water at the time there was a shark on the opposite side of the vessel; a foolish experiment certainly, but the sharks in the Mediterranean were supposed not to be so voracious, or dangerous, as in other climates, which accounted for our being so daring. The doctor often spoke of it afterwards, and used frequently to say to me, "I wonder, Steevens, we could have been guilty of such a piece of utter folly"; for it was certainly fraught with danger, though we had never heard of anyone being attacked by sharks in that latitude. You never can mistake a shark, for he swims with a fin above water. I have often seen them at sea, but never witnessed the capture of one, though we often tried with baited hooks; but they are decidedly not so voracious in the Mediterranean.

The 13th Regiment were quartered on the "Rock" at this time, and the *20th* having been in the West Indies with them some years previously (about 1793 or 1794), they were very attentive and kind, and invited all of us to dinner, which invitation we accepted with much pleasure, and they gave us a most handsome entertainment. The 13th were commanded by the Hon. Colonel Colville;[2] it was a fine regiment and in high order. The meeting of regiments which have become attached to each other is very pleasing and gratifying; frequently they may have not only been in garrison together, but may have also faced the enemy and fought side by side.

We remained a day or two at Gibraltar, and then sailed for our destination, the island of Malta, where we arrived about the end of September or beginning of October, 1803, and found the old *20th* in the garrison of La Valetta, the capital of the island; the regiment was now one battalion, the 2nd battalion having been reduced at the short peace of 1802.

We had plenty of occupation, as far as drilling went, during our stay in Malta; for our Colonel (Ross) used frequently to take the *20th* out into the country at five in the morning, and not bring us home until one p.m. This perhaps may appear to a military man rather exaggerated, but I can vouch for the truth of it, and so can many others. These field-days, drills, or whatever they may be called, were fatiguing in the extreme to us all, particularly to the men, and they were at last discontinued, by an order from the general commanding; these drills were looked upon by our surgeon (my old friend Arnott) as very injurious to the health of the battalion, as the rest of the men was disturbed at the very time they might have had a little sleep, 4 to 5 a.m. being the coolest time of the 24 hours.

I have seen the men of my company with their white trousers quite wet, as if just washed, entirely from excessive perspiration; we were repeatedly out for *eight hours* during the hot weather; frequently crossing the country, scouring the fields over the stone walls, the whole of the regiment acting as light infantry; and *the best* of the *joke* was, that *no other corps in the island was similarly indulged*. We sometimes amused ourselves, in the season, with quail shooting, for the quails at times were very numerous, and afforded the sportsmen much amusement for two or three weeks together. They came over in passes, thousands at a time, from the coast of Africa, and alighted in the island: if the same wind continued, that brought them over, they soon disappeared; but if the wind changed soon after their arrival they then frequently

2. Now (1839) General the Hon. Sir Charles Colville, G.C.B., G.C.H.

34

remained for nearly a month, and we used to be almost tired of roast quail, quail pies, etc., at the mess table.

A party of us once went to the island of Gozo, on an excursion for a week. It was about fifteen or eighteen miles from La Valetta, and we had a detachment there under the command of Captain Bent.[3] Captain Luke Godfrey,[4] 61st Regiment, an old friend of mine and of several others of the *20th*, was likewise of the party; Assist.-Surgeon Miller of my regiment, who was particularly fond of shooting and used to train sporting dogs, was also with us on this excursion of pleasure, besides some more whose names I cannot recollect.

One day, whilst at Gozo, two parties of us were out shooting, and we happened during the day to fall in with each other; and while in conversation, enquiring what sport each party had met with, one of the dogs came to a point, and the rest backed him; there were five dogs, and it so happened they were all of the same litter, and all handsome pointers. To a sportsman's eye this was a beautiful sight; one of the dogs was mine, his name was "Roger."[5] These dogs had all been trained by my old friend and brother officer Miller, who died many years afterwards, surgeon of some regiment. I was always partial to shooting, which makes me rather dwell upon the subject; we had quails and woodcocks in abundance, and after passing a pleasant week at Gozo, those who did not belong to the detachment stationed there returned to the headquarters of our regiment at Malta, sorry at parting with our old friends.

During the time we were quartered at Malta, General Villetta, who commanded, used frequently to invite the officers of the garrison to his table, and there were public and private balls, besides parties and sometimes masquerades. At one of these masquerades, given at the palace, some *20th* officers went as Bacchanalians; they *carried* a donkey up a long flight of stairs[6] and entered the ball room in procession, with

3. Afterwards Major Bent, who was, poor fellow, killed at the head of the *20th* Regiment at the battle of Orthes, 27th February, 1814; he was formerly in the 92nd Regiment, and was with them at the landing in Egypt, 8th March, 1801.
4. Afterwards Major Godfrey, who died in 1837, on half-pay, in Ireland; the 61st and *20th* Regiments were great friends when in garrison together at Malta.
5. Poor "Roger" was shot some years afterwards in England, having shewn symptoms of madness.
6. The animal, frightened at the lights, stubbornly declined to walk up the easy steps, so the pseudo-Bacchanalians, not to be thwarted, carried him up.

one of their number, as Silenus, mounted on the donkey.

We had delightful bathing here, which was very conducive to health, for we required something to brace us during the hot months, the nights in the summer time being very oppressive; for the thermometer was repeatedly as high at twelve o'clock at night as it was at twelve o'clock in the day; at that time, during the day, we generally had a fine breeze, but during the night there was hardly a breath of air, and windows were not closed for months together, as we had no rain nor storms. The wet season was in the spring; the winters were very mild, no frost, and at this time of year a fine climate for delicate constitutions. I have often wondered why invalids do not go to this island during the winter, as steam-packets are only about ten days reaching Malta from England. The thermometer during the hot months was generally from 4° to 88°; frequently day after day about 86.°

CHAPTER 7

Italy & Maida

In the month of March, 1805, we had a great number of Spanish prizes brought into Malta, and at one time there were not less than a hundred sail in the port, some of them very valuable.

We remained in the island till November 3rd, 1805, when we left for Italy to join a Russian army which had gone to that country. After a tedious voyage of about three weeks the troops landed at Castel Amare. The British army fell in with the Russians off Sicily, and we all arrived together, but they disembarked very near Naples, and part of them, I believe, at Capua. We had a very unpleasant march to Nocera after we landed; the roads were very wet, and we did not reach the place until ten o'clock p.m., and afterwards had a great difficulty to procure quarters.

While we were in this country we received an order to meet the Russians (about 20,000 men), and to be reviewed by the King of Naples, and a tiring day we had of it; we left our quarters about five a.m., on the 30th November, and had eight or ten miles to go to the ground, situate on the sea shore not far distant from the foot of Mount Vesuvius; the whole of the beach for miles was covered with ashes from the mountain, and it was hard work getting through it, particularly after our march from Nocera; here we waited six hours before his Neapolitan Majesty made his appearance, which was about one p.m. At last the sound of bugles and beating of drums, for the men to fall in, gave us notice of His Majesty's approach, and a miserable set out it was; the traces of the carriage were merely ropes, so different to what I was accustomed to see in my own country, and particularly when royalty appeared; and I do not recollect that there were more than two or three carriages in his retinue.

After the Russian and our army had passed the King in review order, (which of course took some time, for all the officers had to salute His Majesty,) we returned to our respective quarters, which I recollect we did not reach much before nine o'clock p.m.; a pretty sharp day's work, and all to gratify the whim of a macaroni King. While we were waiting for His Majesty, the men piled their arms and lay down, (fortunately it was a fine October day), for they and all of us were tired with the worry of waiting; being six hours behind time it was a bad sample of punctuality; besides, neither officers nor men took any provisions with them, so that we were without any food from six in the morning until nine at night, having had nothing but grumbling to feast upon, which is said to be a soldier's privilege.

The King of Naples was a very good-looking man, and his Queen also was a fine old woman; one of the Princesses I thought rather handsome, and the young Prince very much so. We found this country much colder than Malta, and the tops of the surrounding mountains were frequently covered with snow. As there were no barracks here, we were quartered in private houses. I lived, with some officers, in a gentleman's house about a mile from Nocera, and the family were very civil to us; at these houses they gave us lodging only.

After marching and counter-marching for a few weeks, without seeing the enemy or even smelling powder, we left the country and proceeded to the island of Sicily, where we disembarked a day or two after we arrived off Messina, and went into several different quarters close at hand; and, soon after, we were stationed along the coast, the Faro of Messina, as far as the Light House, which was opposite Scylla Rock, the spot of the celebrated Charybdis. We were in these quarters a few months, and were then ordered on the expedition to Calabria, under Major-General Stuart.

About the 30th of June we embarked in large open boats, called *feluccas*, and were employed cruising off that part of Calabria which lay between Reggio and Cape Spartivento; the boats, on an emergency, could hold about one hundred men, but we had not more than one officer and about eighteen or twenty men in each, so, with respect to our force, we deceived the French General (Regnier) and his army very much. We were out off that part of the coast, not with any intention of landing, but merely to draw the attention of the French there, whilst our army landed at the Bay of St. Euphemia.

At the expiration of four days we returned to Messina harbour, quitted our boats, and on the 3rd of July (1806) we embarked in transports and immediately set sail for the rest of the army. We anchored in the Bay of St. Euphemia early on the morning of the 4th; while we lay at anchor the Admiral, Sir Sydney Smith, hailed the ships, saying it was General Stuart's intention to attack the enemy that very morning.

Without waiting for orders, our gallant chief, Colonel Ross, gave directions for the regiment to disembark soon after daylight. General Stuart had landed with a small army a few days previously and they were now engaged, for we could hear the firing and see the smoke; we therefore cheerfully obeyed the order and landed forthwith, after filling our haversacks and canteens, for officers as well as men carried their three days' provisions, and their blankets and change of linen. In landing, the boats had to go through a great deal of surf, and the men spoilt all their cartridges, but having some casks of ammunition in the boats, we soon replenished their pouches, and immediately hurried across the country, through woods and marshes, in the direction whence the music of cannon and musketry was heard, and we reached our little army just at the. very: nick of time, for we came through a wood upon the left of the British line, which the French cavalry were trying to turn.

We immediately formed, and they attempted to charge us to turn our left; but Colonel Ross threw back the left wing of the old *20th*, that they might not get round our flank; and, after giving them a few shots, they relinquished the attempt; for a long time, however, they kept hovering about us, and made us change our position several times; but we were always ready to receive them. The enemy's infantry suffered severely in this action, called the Battle of Maida, but their cavalry seemed afraid to engage, though we had none of that arm.

Our army consisted of about 4000 men, and the French had between 7000 and 8000 in this engagement, including some hundreds of cavalry. The French were in a strong position on a hill, but their commander, General Regnier, fancied he could easily drive us into the sea; he therefore left his position, attacked our army, and got well thrashed; for the number of French killed, wounded, and prisoners amounted to nearly our whole force; the field of battle the next morning was a scene awful to behold, dead and wounded lying together by hundreds.

The Light Infantry Battalion, (composed of ten light companies from several regiments, including that of the *20th* under Captain Murdoch McLean,) commanded by Colonel Kempt,[1] was on the right of the line, and was very warmly engaged with the enemy, particularly with the French Regiment *Le Premier Leger,* which was nearly annihilated by a charge of our Light Infantry Battalion and suffered great loss, as acknowledged by one of the French officers who was taken prisoner. In this bloody combat these two regiments advanced towards each other, without firing, until they came within pistol shot; our Light Battalion then gave them a volley, and the commanding officer (Kempt), seizing a favourable opportunity, charged and routed them most completely.

In this gallant struggle poor Captain McLean of the *20th* was mortally wounded, and did not survive five minutes; we were most attached friends, having been brother officers for ten years, and had passed many happy years in each other's society; there was but one day's difference in our ages: I greatly regretted his loss, and so did many others, as he was much liked in the old regiment: he was a brave fellow, and, I believe, lost his life by his gallantry. It was after the French left had been thus thoroughly beaten, that they tried to bring up their right to turn the British left, but, as previously described, the opportune arrival of the old *20th* frustrated this attempt.

It was very remarkable that, considering the large number of officers who fell on the side of the enemy, the British had but *one* officer (Captain McClean) *killed in the field* on this day; there were many officers and men wounded, and many men killed, but nothing in comparison with what the French lost. Major Powlett, who was attached to the Light Infantry Battalion, was very severely wounded.[2]

---

1. Afterwards the Right Hon. Sir James Kempt, G.C.B., G.C.H., a Lieut.-General and Master-General of the Ordnance.

2. Major Henry Powlett belonged to the 44th Regiment; he had previously served many years in the *20th* Regiment, in which he attained the rank of Major, and was appointed to the 44th Regiment on the formation of the 2nd Battalion, in July, 1803. He died many years afterwards a Lieut.-Colonel on half-pay, and Lieut.-Governor of Carisbrooke Castle.

So terminated the glorious Battle of Maida; we did not pursue the enemy on their retreating, as our force was too weak, and, besides, it was not our policy to do so; but we bivouacked not far from the scene of action.

I recollect one night, while on bivouac, a large snake crawled over me; we were at the time lying down in high grass; I felt most uncomfortable afterwards, and hardly closed my eyes again that night.[3]

At the close of this campaign fever broke out amongst the troops, and carried off many officers and men; it was not infectious, but was brought on by over fatigue. I escaped, fortunately, and was perfectly well during all our fatiguing marches over the mountains; we did not have our clothes off for some weeks, sleeping in the open fields under trees.

Whilst in Calabria we marched to Reggio and one or two other places, and, after being in that country about a month or so, we returned to Sicily, leaving a garrison at Scylla, opposite the Faro Tower, on the other side of the Straits of Messina; I think Major David Walker[4] of the *20th* was left in command of the garrison. Upon our return to Sicily we were quartered at Messina.

After the death of Captain McLean, the light company was commanded by Captain Colborne, and in the autumn of 1806, after he was put upon the Staff, I took the command of this company, and joined them at Contessa, not far from Messina, where the Light Infantry Battalion was quartered, still under the command of Colonel Kempt; and in that corps was my old chum, Charley Blomer, at that time in the light company of the 31st Regiment; naturally enough we saw a great deal of each other, and passed many happy hours together.

One day a party of four of us visited Mount Etna; it took us nearly a week to get from Messina to the top and back again, the distance being about ninety miles. From Catania to the top is about thirty miles, and all up hill; rather fatiguing, but we rode the whole of the way, except two miles, when we were obliged to walk, as the ground was too steep for riding. It was a very pleasant ride going through the different regions; first of all the "ashy," then the "fertile," afterwards the

---

3. The field of Maida was covered with myrtle bushes, and for many years the officers and men of the *20th* used always to near a sprig of myrtle in their caps on the 4th of July, the anniversary of this glorious victory.

4. Afterwards Lieut.-Colonel 58th Regiment, and now (1839) a Major-General.

"woody," and last of all the "snowy region." I found it excessively cold going up, for I rode fully two miles on snow, and then had to walk up the steepest part of the mountain on snow; only three of us reached the top.

The weather became very bad while we were at the summit, and it was with difficulty that we found our way down again; then came on a very heavy fall of snow, and the wind blew pretty hard; the guide was so alarmed that he did not go as far with us as he ought; but we were determined to see all we could. There was so much smoke issuing from the crater, that I only once saw down into it, and now and then I heard a kind of rumbling noise, but the mountain that day was reckoned very quiet; I was so much gratified with the sight that I should have liked to have gone again.

During our stay at Messina we had several severe shocks of earthquake; one shock cracked the wall of my bedroom from the ceiling to the floor, and down to the bottom of the room underneath.

I was in the Light Infantry Battalion a few months, and was then ordered to join my regiment at Messina, it being about to move to Milazzo in another part of the island. We did not find Milazzo healthy, and at one time while there we had nearly half our officers and about 300 men ill. I suffered a good deal from a swelling in the knee, which I believe was rheumatic; I was lame for months, but with the immediate prospect of active service, I did not like to go away for a change. We had a very hot summer here, thermometer, with a sea breeze, sometimes as high as 97° in my room; even the inhabitants felt the heat very much, and used to sleep on the flat roof (terrace) of their houses; one day when the *sirocco*, a hot wind, blew, the thermometer in my room rose to 100°.

During the month of April, 1807, while at Milazzo, we heard that Admiral Sir John Duckworth had forced the passage of the Dardanelles, when the *Ajax* was accidentally blown up, having caught fire at night; the captain, several officers, and about 400 men were saved; a great many were lost in consequence of their jumping overboard at the commencement of the accident; and, as it was blowing hard, and was likewise dark at the time, they were unable to reach the other ships, or to get on shore. The passage which the Admiral forced was very narrow, and the batteries were blazing at him in all directions; but what did it avail? the "wooden walls" were not at all damaged.

We remained at Milazzo till the autumn of 1807, and then embarked for Lisbon with some other troops, under the command of Sir John Moore;[5] we did not land there, (as I believe the French had got possession of the place before us,) but made sail for old England: we disembarked at Portsmouth in January, 1808, and marched to Brabourne Lees Barracks, in Kent.

---

5. Killed at the battle of Corunna, January 16th, 1809.

CHAPTER 8

The Peninsular War

It was reported, on our arrival at Spithead, that we were to be sent back again, as Sir John Moore had brought us home without orders; however, it was thought better of, and we were allowed to land, but I fancy it was rather doubtful whether we ought not have been sent back again on our first arrival, which would have been a very great disappointment to us all, as the regiment had been up the Mediterranean about eight years, and some of the other troops about the same time; but our stay at home was very short, for it will be seen that we were off about six months after. We remained at Brabourne Lees barracks but a short time, and then marched to Colchester barracks, in Essex, continued there a few weeks and then went to Ipswich barracks, and from thence, in the month of August, to Harwich, where we embarked and sailed once more for Portugal. It was a most sultry day when the troops marched to Harwich; many of the men were quite overcome with the excessive heat; some men of the 2nd (or Queen's) Regiment died in consequence of the hot weather.

There were at that time a great many young men in the "Queen's" who were not able to go through as much fatigue as the old soldiers of the *20th* could bear, which accounted for the casualties.

On the 20th of August, 1808, we disembarked at Maceira, near Peniche, and lay on the beach that night, and the following morning we took part in the Battle of Vimiera; we were in Major-General Ackland's Brigade, and the army was commanded by Sir Arthur Wellesley.[1]

---

1. Sir Arthur used afterwards often to speak of the Battle of Vimiera, and seemed to talk of this action with much pleasure, it being one of the first engagements, in Europe, where he commanded.

The old 50th were much engaged in this action, and behaved very gallantly. Only part of the *20th* were present at the Battle of Vimiera, under the command of Lieut.-Colonel Campbell, as headquarters could not land for want of boats; all on board were dreadfully annoyed, when they heard the firing, that they could not join the remainder of their comrades; but such is the fate of war.

I was detached during the action and was with two companies of the 95th (Rifles)[2] we were engaged in driving some French riflemen out of a wood that was in front of the centre of our army; my company (the light company) behaved nobly on the occasion; I had only one man wounded; we knocked over several of the enemy, and took many prisoners; the French hid themselves behind the trees and kept up a very heavy fire, but we advanced on them very rapidly, and drove them away in all directions, pouring in volley after volley of musketry. Several pieces of cannon were taken that day, and the French lost an immense number of men. We had one officer killed, Lieut. Brooke, and one officer wounded, Lieut. Hogge.[3] I was excessively ill during the action, and suffered a great deal of pain; but having command of the Light Company I could not bear the idea of being left on board ship, so I landed with my men, and got through the fatigue of that day better than I expected.

The French at Vimiera were commanded by Junot, and they were completely beaten in all points.

We were encamped afterwards at Becarinha, near Cintra, not far from Lisbon. We were hutted when we could get wood, otherwise we were exposed to all weathers, never taking off our clothes.

The army in and about Lisbon was under the command of Sir Hugh Dalrymple, as, after the action. Sir Arthur was superseded in his command, two Generals, Sir Harry Burrard and Sir Hugh Dalrymple, having been sent out from England; both, I believe, were senior to Sir Arthur Wellesley; and then that unfortunate Convention of Cintra was entered into. I call it *unfortunate*, because the very garrison of Lisbon, under Junot, who were allowed to embark for their own country although prisoners of war, opposed our army again in Spain soon after.

---

2. Belonging to the 1st Battalion 95th, and attached to General Ackland's Brigade, *vide* Sir W. Cope's *History of the Rifle Brigade* (also published by Leonaur.)
3. Now (1839) Lieut.-Colonel, Unattached.

It was a great pity that Convention was ever concluded, as no doubt if Sir Arthur Wellesley had not been superseded in his command, the result would have been very different; the army was very much dissatisfied, and indeed so were the people in England, at the French garrison being allowed to escape, consisting, as it did, of many thousand men; if our army had advanced and attacked Lisbon, not a man of them would have escaped, but they must all have been taken prisoners.

After this treaty was concluded we moved from our encampment at Becarinha on our way to Elvas, my regiment having been ordered there, and we were the first English regiment ever quartered in that place; on our march we crossed the Tagus to Aldea Galega, then to Canya, Montemore Nuevo, Vende de Duc, Aryolas, Estremos, Alberoca, Villa Vicosa, and from thence to Elvas, the frontier town of Portugal. At Estremos the inhabitants were particularly civil and kind to the regiment; they made us a present of a couple of fine bullocks, and gave fruit, wine, bread, etc., to the men as well as to the officers. The bullocks' horns were decorated with ribbons, and they were driven out of the town at the head of the regiment.

We remained at Villa Vicosa a few days, and, during our stay, we received a handsome present from the Lady Abbess and nuns, and were invited to go into the convent there. The present consisted of two large dishes of sweetmeats and cakes, ornamented with coloured cut paper, flowers, etc.; they were beautifully arranged, and of course very sweet, and were a delightful treat to us. We were very politely received by the Lady Abbess on our entering the convent, and we thought it a high honour to be admitted within the walls. We sat chatting to the Lady Abbess and the young nuns, for many of them spoke French as also Italian; I managed to get on pretty well with the French language, for foreigners will always help you out when you are at fault.

Many of the nuns were both young and handsome, and we thought it was a great pity to see so many fine young women excluded from society; but they appeared cheerful and happy, and were particularly pleasant and agreeable in conversation, and we were very sorry when the time came for our departure; we used, now and then, afterwards, to go and talk to them through the iron grating, but, if I recollect well, the Lady Abbess was always present.

While at Villa Vicosa I amused myself fishing in a pond, close to the palace where I was quartered. I fished out of one of the windows, and my tackle was not much suited to the angler, for it consisted of a piece of stick for a rod, and a string with a crooked pin tied to it; however, one of my subalterns, Harding (whom I have mentioned before), managed to catch a dish of fish now and then with my assistance; but I am almost ashamed to say what they were,—nothing more nor less than *gold and silver fish*. One day our little mess gave a dish of these fish, for a fore-quarter of mutton, to another mess; for we could not all meet at one dinner, but generally a company or two of officers dined together, as we used frequently to do on service.

Part of the regiment was quartered at Elvas, and part at Fort La Lippe. The inhabitants of Elvas were particularly friendly and attentive to us; and, never having seen a British regiment before, they made much of the old *20th*. Our Colonel (Ross) speaking the language of the country, and also French, very fluently, was a great advantage. Previous to our occupying Fort La Lippe the French had a garrison there, but, being included in the Convention of Cintra, they marched out soon after our arrival at Elvas, and were escorted to Lisbon to join their own army there, and, I believe, opposed us again some months after in Spain. At Elvas I was billeted at a gentleman's house; the family consisted of himself, wife, and daughter. The daughter had a very pretty black horse, which I wanted to purchase; her father was not unwilling, if she were inclined to part with it, as it was entirely at her own disposal, and I often asked her to let me have the horse. One day I was talking to Colonel Ross about it, he immediately said, "Shew her twenty guineas, and the horse is yours;" dollars were not so tempting as guineas; nothing like the old guinea with the head of good old George III upon it; that coin passed everywhere.

As I had nothing but dollars Colonel Ross lent me the twenty guineas; I laid them on the table before the young lady, and the black horse was immediately mine. The little horse afterwards met with a sad fate, having been one of the number that were shot near Corunna just before that action, more of which affair will be mentioned hereafter. Here, as at Villa Vicosa, we used to chat with the nuns through the iron grating, and one of our officers (Lieut. W——) a handsome young fellow, fell in love with one of them, a very pretty girl; the affection seemed reciprocal, and, I believe, they were both equally sorry when the regiment marched away.

We afterwards moved into Fort La Lippe; it was a very strong place, stood high above the town of Elvas, and opposite (at about six or eight miles distance) was Badajos, the frontier town of Spain, a fortified place; at this time it was not in the possession of the French, but was garrisoned by the Spaniards. Fort La Lippe was a fine healthy situation, from which we had a very extensive view, both of Spain and Portugal: while we were here our horses were taken to water, down the hill outside the fort, to a cistern of fine spring water: for some days I found my horse bled very much at the mouth; on examination it was ascertained to be caused by leeches, several having been found about his tongue.

After being quartered at this Fort some little time we marched thence into Spain. Our first day's march was to Campo Mayor in Estremadura, and from thence to Albuquerque, Alcede, Brosas, Alcantara, Sazza Mayor, Morilezza, Perales, Penio Pardas, in old Castile, and Guinelda to Ciudad Rodrigo, where we remained some little time; it was a large fortified place, and two or three years afterwards was once more garrisoned by the French, and stormed and taken by our troops, but the old *20th* were not at that time in the country. From Ciudad Rodrigo we were ordered to Salamanca, and marched to San Martini del Rio, and to Canillas di Abaxo, and from thence to Salamanca. On our route from Fort La Lippe to Salamanca, we passed through an extensive forest; it was nearly two days' march to get through it, and the first night we halted at a small village in the middle of the forest, I think it was Perales or Penio Pardas, but I am not certain. There were many wolves about at night, and the people were obliged to shut up their horses, cattle, etc., after dark, for they had been known to eat part of an animal alive.

We remained at Salamanca for some weeks, awaiting the arrival of the remainder of our troops, which, from the force being so large, were obliged to march by different routes. When collected we mustered,— including cavalry and artillery,—40,000 men. We experienced some fatiguing marches between Lisbon and Salamanca, nearly 400 miles; I marched on foot all the time, and I never had better health. Sir John Moore was in command of the Army, and we thought ourselves very fortunate in having so fine a fellow at our head.

Salamanca was a large town on the river Tormes, over which there was a handsome bridge to enter the town; it contained a fine Cathedral and several Colleges, but the streets were very narrow and dirty. In the river was a bird called a diver, which afforded some of us a little amusement; he used to be close to the town, and some of the inhabitants related an odd story about this diver, which they called by the name of "Buonaparte"; they said it had been there about twenty years, and no one could shoot it.

One morning three of us, poor Bent, Harding, (both no more) and I, took our fowling pieces, determined, if possible, to shoot this celebrated bird; we found him on the river, and so placed ourselves that, whenever he came up after diving, he was always between us. We got several shots at him, but he was always so quick in getting under water after the trigger was pulled, that we never could touch him; and, after firing until our patience was quite exhausted, we gave it up. Others, besides ourselves, were equally unsuccessful at various times; so we left him as we found him, and when we quitted Salamanca "Buonaparte" was still alive. If we had had detonating locks no doubt we should have bagged him, in spite of the superstitious notions many had concerning this bird.

At Salamanca I was billeted at the house of a Spanish gentleman, who drove six mules in his carriage, and seemed a person of good fortune; but whether *Tory* or *Radical* I know not, but I should rather suppose the latter, for he never paid me a visit, nor shewed me any attention. One of the six mules, which this Spanish gentleman drove in his carriage, stood so high in the shoulder, that I had the curiosity to measure him by my own height, and I found that his shoulder came to the top of my light infantry cap, and I stood 5ft. 11 in. without it; so I conclude that the animal must have been nearly as high as the celebrated horse, exhibited in England in 1837, which measured twenty hands. The mule I have mentioned was much higher than either of the other five, but it was by no means a handsome or well-proportioned animal.

In the meadows round about Salamanca were immense quantities of mushrooms; we could have gathered bushels of them: we used to have them stewed, boiled, and cooked in various ways. I cannot exactly say how long we remained at Salamanca, but it was a few weeks;

and it was reported that our retreat was finally decided upon before we marched from that place, for the Spaniards gave us no support, and their soldiers were sneaking away to their homes in all directions,— frequently a dozen or twenty together,—leaving us to fight their battles; and without their assistance our force was too small to cope with the enemy, for we had not more than 24,000 men afterwards at Corunna, and the French had about 40,000,—very great odds; still, as will be seen, we were conquerors in that action.

CHAPTER 9

Retreat

As soon as we moved from Salamanca it was looked upon then as the commencement of Sir John Moore's retreat, as it was called.[1] From Salamanca we went to Castilianos di Morisco, Christofal di Cuesta, Villa Excusa, Toro, Pedrosa del Rey, Tedra, Villapando, Valdieras, Santi-erbo, Graghal di los Campos, Mayorga, Fuente sa Bucco, Benevente, Lavaniessa, Astorga, Combaros, Bembibre, Calcavelos, Villa Franca, Ferrareas, Nogales, Constantino, Lugo; and from thence we marched one league to Milarosa, where we took up a position on high ground, a commanding situation, and the French were in a position just op-posite to us. We remained one whole day there, expecting the enemy would attack us, but we only looked at each other, and not a shot was fired on either side. As soon as night came on we retired about three leagues, and took up another position, and I think it was in this posi-tion that we had a little skirmishing, the French having attacked us, but it was very trifling.

From thence we went to Cordeda and then to Monillos, which was about a league from Corunna; here our Brigade remained a day or two, and the other part of the army was cantoned in and about Corunna, as the ships, that were expected for us, had not arrived; otherwise it was intended that the army should have embarked im-mediately on their arrival at Corunna; but being delayed the French had plenty of time to bring up their force; we were therefore obliged to take up a position. We suffered great privations during the retreat, which was seriously commenced on Christmas Day, 1808; and from that time until the battle of Corunna, January 16th, 1809, the enemy

1. *Vide* Appendix "B."

51

kept pretty close to us, and at times harassed us a good deal. We were very frequently within musket shot of each other, and occasionally had a brush with them.

On the evening of Christmas Day I recollect going through a stream of water, and rather a deep one; we might just as well have gone over a small bridge close at hand, for we got wet to our waists and had no opportunity of drying our clothes, and this on a Christmas evening (when our friends at home were enjoying themselves at their firesides) was no joke; but General Anstruther, who gave the order, thought it would have caused too great a delay to take the troops over so narrow a bridge; however I was none the worse, being of an age at this time to go through a great deal.

On this same day we lost one of our men In a melancholy way, and a fine young man he was; he was in the Grenadier Company; he was eating a piece of roll or new bread, while walking along and talking to his comrades on the march, when part of it stuck in his throat and choked him. Our excellent kind Surgeon (Arnott)[2] was called immediately to his assistance, but could not save him, and the poor man was soon after buried.

One day I recollect there was a little skirmish with the enemy, for, after the excessive fatigue we underwent, we were obliged occasionally to halt to recruit ourselves, and then the French used to attack us. On this occasion they had a party led on by an officer on a grey horse; a man of the 95th Rifles fired at him, and he was seen to fall. Colonel Ross, and all of us who witnessed it, were very sorry, as he seemed to be a remarkably gallant fellow; but such, alas! is the fate of war.[3]

2. Surgeon Archibald Arnott was for many years in the *20th* Regiment, and served with it during various campaigns. He was with the regiment at St Helena at the time the Emperor Napoleon was there, and had the honour of attending the illustrious captive during his latter days. Napoleon on his deathbed desired that his gold snuff-box might be brought to him, when, with his dying hand, he scratched on the lid, with a penknife, the letter "N," and presented it to Surgeon Arnott as a parting memento of his esteem and gratitude.

3. This officer was no doubt General Colbert, who commanded the advanced guard of the French cavalry, the circumstances of whose death are mentioned in Sir William Cope's *History of the Rifle Brigade* (also published by Leonaur in two volumes, vol. 1 *The 95th Rifles*.) where we read that on the 3rd January, 1809, when the 95th formed the rear-guard of the reserve, during the retreat of Sir John Moore, they were attacked, near the village of Calcavelos, by the enemy's cavalry under General Colbert, when Thomas Plunket, (continued next page.)

The French had much the advantage of us in these petty warfares, for I have frequently seen their light troops mounted behind their dragoons, so that when they came to a favourable place to make an attack, these fellows dismounted quite fresh, and our light troops, who had been always marching, had to oppose them; still we managed to beat them off.

At a place called, I think, Calcavelos, a soldier of one of the regiments, who was a straggler and had been taken prisoner, managed to get again into our lines, although severely wounded in several places; his wounds being chiefly about his face and arms, he was, poor fellow, able to walk, but the French cavalry had cut him about terribly; he was a dreadful object to look at, and greatly to be pitied, though perhaps his condition had been brought on him by his own irregularities; still we could not help feeling for him. Colonel Ross led him through the ranks of our regiment, to point out to the men the way in which the French would serve them, if they lagged behind through drunkenness, I believe the poor sufferer, after all, was left behind a day or two after, as we had not the means to carry him on; and, in all probability, the surgeon said, he would not survive, as he had so many wounds. It was, supposed he had been drunk when taken prisoner, and, having resisted, no doubt the enemy ill-used him, for many hundreds of stragglers who reached our lines, and had been prisoners, were not at all mutilated.

It was at this same town (Calcavelos), I think, that I met with a radical priest, who treated the French very differently from our troops; but he paid for his folly. We had been quartered in this priest's house, but the men of my company had been indifferently accommodated, having no straw in their rooms; and when I remonstrated with this priest, he said that he could not procure any straw, so we were obliged to go without; but he appeared very civil, and I concluded that it was out of his power to make our rooms more comfortable.

We marched out of the town to continue our retreat, but unexpectedly we were ordered to return, and the different companies of

---

a private of the 96th, noted for his excellent shooting, shot the French General dead. Napier, in his *Peninsular War*, writing of the incident, observes, "his fine martial figure, his voice, his gestures, and, above all, his great valour, had excited the admiration of the British, and a general feeling of sorrow was predominant when the gallant soldier fell" the regiment were directed to occupy their old quarters; I took my Light Company back to the priest's house, and lo! and behold! all the rooms were knee-deep in straw, as the French were expected in the town that day, if we had not returned; of course my men were very much exasperated against the priest for his deceitful conduct, so I was determined to punish him in some way; the priest himself was not forthcoming, as you may well suppose. He happened to have a little store of bacon in the house, so I had a piece served out to each of my men, and after all, I believe, it was no great loss to him, for no doubt the French would have helped themselves to it as soon as they arrived, as was generally their plan; except in this instance, we always paid for what we had; and the night before I had paid the priest for a pint of wine and some bacon for each man, but after his behaviour I think he was rightly served.

We suffered a good deal from fatigue, wet, and cold, besides the want of provisions. One day I had nothing to eat but a few raw turnips. The chief brunt of the retreat fell upon us, the regiments composing the reserve under the command of General Paget.[4]

I commanded the Light Company of the old *20th*; a fine company it was, and I was not a little proud of them. The regiments took the duty of rear-guard alternately. One day I was in the rear of all our troops, with my Light Company and my two subalterns, Lieuts. Lutyens and Harding;[5] we had a large medicine chest in charge, which I had orders to destroy, if the bullocks, that were drawing it, knocked up, which unfortunately turned out to be the case. This detained us some time, the chest being so well and closely packed, for it was just as It came from Apothecaries' Hall, and was very valuable. The chest was taken out of the cart, and every bottle, jar, case, etc., thrown out of it and broken to pieces, the men using stones and the butt-ends of their firelocks; we afterwards destroyed the chest itself by jumping upon it;

---

4. Consisting of the *20th*, 28th, 52nd, Gist, and 96th Regiments and some artillery; whether there were any more regiments in the reserve I cannot exactly recollect.
5. Lieut. Latyens died on board ship, many years afterwards, when coming home from the East Indies; he was then a captain in the 20th Regiment; and Lieut. Harding was afterwards captain in the Cape Corps, and died at the Cape a magistrate; we had passed many happy years together. When I think of my old regiment it often cause s painful reflections, so many of my old friends and companions in the 20th being no more.

in short, I do not think we left anything, worth having, for the enemy when they came up, which they did very soon after we retired.

We were often within shot of the enemy's first file of dragoons, but we did not fire at each other, our object being to reach Corunna as expeditiously as possible, and to avoid engaging, our army being so inferior in point of numbers, for the strength of the French was about double ours.

At a place called Nogales, on our retreat, there was a bridge to be blown up, and my company were nearly taken prisoners, through some mistake with respect to an order. I received orders to post my men on the side of the bridge next the enemy, so as to cover it, whilst preparations were being made for blowing it up. However, by some mistake they forgot to recall us, and we anxiously listened for bugle signal; still no sound. At last one of my subalterns (Harding) said to me he thought we ought to retire, or we should be left behind; for I was told before we took up our position, that we should be there but a short time. I took his advice and immediately made for the bridge, the advance-guard of the French cavalry being but a short distance from us, but they did not pursue us.

We retreated in double quick time, and it was fortunate we did so, for, as soon as we had crossed the bridge, our engineer (Captain Paisley I believe) blew it up; if the bridge had been blown up a few minutes earlier we should have been just in time to be too late, and many of us might have been taken prisoners; however, at any rate, we should have tried the river, which would have been the only chance of escaping.

During the retreat Captain Byron commanded the Grenadier Company of the *20th*, and we used often to say, "who will knock up first, the Grenadiers or Light Bobs?" He soon gave in and went on board ship on the sick-list; Lieut. Telford was one of his subalterns.[6]

The French were not much impeded by the bridge at Nogales being blown up, for they discovered a ford not a great way from the bridge, and their cavalry soon overtook us, and frequently harassed us a good deal.

We witnessed many painful sights; it was dreadful to see the num-

6. He, poor fellow, now (1839) lies in Cheltenham Churchyard, having died a Captain on half-pay.

bers of dead lying by the roadside, consisting of men, and sometimes women and children; once or twice I saw a little infant lying close to its mother, both dead; also horses, asses, mules, and oxen, some frozen to death, having been overcome by fatigue; others were shot, for the orders were that whenever any of the animals were unable to proceed, they were to be made away with.

Several officers of my own regiment were walking without shoes, but fortunately we came to a place where we had some stores under the charge of a commissary, and those who were in want of shoes supplied themselves. I threw away an old pair and got new ones, but the exchange, though necessary, was not a very agreeable one, for I suffered very very much from my new shoes being too large and from their being so thick, as they were what we soldiers called am-munition-shoes, being intended for the men. We likewise supplied ourselves with some salt provisions and whatever we could take with us. We set fire to everything left behind, and some little time after we had quitted the place—for it was towards night when we moved on—we could see the fire raging, most likely in possession of the French, for they were always pretty close to us, and annoyed us whenever an opportunity offered.

We were repeatedly soaked with rain, and had no opportunity to change our clothes. I have sometimes had my joints nearly stiff" with wet and cold, still my health continued perfectly good; but I have often thought that if the retreat had lasted many days longer, I should have been completely done up, for most of us had gone through al-most as much as we were able to contend with; we were nearly all young men, but still our privations were very trying. The regiment used sometimes to march left in front, and one day as I was walking alongside Colonel Ross, at the head of the regiment, I observed that he frequently fell fast asleep and nearly fell off his horse, being almost worn out. I also was so over fatigued that I very often fell asleep as I walked along, waking up to find myself in rear of the regiment; thus adding considerably to my fatigues, by having to work my way up to the front again.

I recollect one day we took up our position to cover the retreat of the stragglers, which at this time, it was supposed, consisted of about 1500 or 2000 men. It was a dreadfully wet day, and our limbs were stiff with wet and the extreme cold and severity of the weather. On this day many hundreds of the stragglers came in; some who had been left behind through fatigue and sickness, and many—too many—who had strayed through drunkenness; one man, who was supposed to have been dipping his canteen into a large butt of wine, was actually drowned in it. The scenes of drunkenness were truly appalling, such I never before nor since witnessed, but it was chiefly among the young soldiers, who landed at Corunna and came out to join our army.

Our regiment lost hardly any men, for they were generally between the ages of twenty-five and thirty-five, and able to go through a great deal of fatigue; besides, our Colonel (poor Ross) gave orders, that whenever we did happen to get into a town, the officers were not to go to their billets, but to remain with their men; the consequence was that we were always a check upon our men, and prevented them from drinking, for of course they liked a buck-horn of wine as well as any other soldiers; and also, if we had been called upon in the night, we were then always ready to turn out with our different companies.

Our stragglers being so numerous, and being of course armed, the enemy did not venture to attack them; however, one day the French seemed to be making some demonstration for an attack, and a sergeant,—I believe one of the 43rd Regiment,—formed up the men and made a good fight of it, beating off the enemy. I heard afterwards that he was very properly rewarded by promotion, for he displayed much judgment and coolness with his bravery, and was, no doubt, by his skill and valour, the cause of many stragglers rejoining their regiments.[7]

One day, in consequence of the oxen being overcome with fatigue while drawing a cart laden with dollars, we were obliged to throw the money away, amounting to about £25,000; it happened that, at the time we were throwing the money away, we were in a high situation, that part of the road being upon a hill and perfectly visible to the enemy. It was an unpleasant sight for us to see the little casks of dollars thrown down the slope into the valley on the side of the road, some of them breaking, when out flew the dollars in all directions. Many

7. In the Historical Records of the 43rd Regiment, by Sir R. G. A. Levinge, Bart., it is stated that this sergeant's name was William Newman, 2nd Battalion 43rd regiment, and that for his conspicuous gallantry on this occasion he was appointed ensign in the 1st West India Regiment.

of the soldiers' wives went into the valley and loaded themselves with dollars, and several were, in consequence, taken prisoners; the French, not allowing any women to be with their army, sent them back into our lines in double-quick, *but without the money.*

There ought not to have been any women with our army, after we commenced our retreat. Our women received a liberal allowance to pay their way back to Lisbon; but, after being absent a few days, they again made their appearance, and many of them, poor things, perished. One I recollect perfectly well, from being a particularly well-conduct-ed woman; she had been with the *20th* Regiment about eleven years, and was of a delicate constitution, so that she was unable to undergo the hardships to which she was subjected. She was missed during the retreat; it appeared that her daughter—quite a young girl—lost her mother in the dark one night, and never heard of her again. I have said a good deal about this person, as her mistress at Liverpool—where she lived as servant—spoke of her in the highest terms, and was sorry she married a soldier. Her end was certainly an unfortunate one, but she was an example of good conduct.

The money, which we had thrown away, was soon in the possession of the French, and fine pickings they had; £25,000 was no bad haul for a morning's work.

Previous to the money being thrown away, it was proposed, I heard, that the officers and men should carry a certain number of dollars, but whether from being so hard pressed by the enemy, we had not time to distribute the money, or whether the men were unwilling to carry it, I cannot exactly say; but I believe that the latter was the case, for everyone seemed so fatigued that they wanted no additional weight to carry. For my own part I should have been sorry to have carried even twenty or thirty dollars in my pocket, (such were my feelings at the time,) wishing to keep myself as light as I could, and I am sure many were of my opinion.

We had a great laugh, a year or two afterwards, at several officers of my regiment who were very zealous in carrying some dollars; they little thought Government would have called upon them to return what they had received, for the money must have been lost if they had not carried it. However, one morning (I may say one *gloomy* morn-ing), very unexpectedly, an order was received for the refunding of the whole of the money with which these *zealous* officers had trudged along the road many a weary hour, and they were obliged to hand out what they had received, and *might think themselves lucky they had not the interest to pay*; of course it was a great inconvenience to many, and a great annoyance to all, to refund money they had every reason to suppose was their own.

During the retreat a little boy was found, whose parents were supposed to have perished. I think he was picked up by Colonel Ross, for I recollect perfectly well seeing him with a child in front of his saddle, but whether or not this little boy was the same I cannot exactly say. This orphan was taken care of by our regiment and brought to England, and one of the soldiers (an armourer I recollect he was, but I forget his name) adopted him, and treated him as his own child. After a few years the poor orphan died, much to the grief of the worthy philanthropic soldier. I had often seen the boy in the barracks; he was well taken care of and was very well behaved, and the man who adopted him was much attached to him.

Among the numerous things that were destroyed during our retreat, was one which most of the officers were sorry to part with; it was our big drum, and a most excellent one it was, being a very fine mellow-toned instrument; as it was thought very cumbersome to carry our colonel gave orders to have it destroyed; no sooner said than done; the drum was broken to pieces by jumping upon it. It seemed a pity to destroy it, for we never had a good one afterwards, and we often regretted when our band was playing that we had not our old drum, the sound of which we had heard for years on many a day's march, and on many a parade, both abroad and at home.

CHAPTER 10

Corunna

While we were in the neighbourhood of Corunna an immense magazine of gunpowder (4000 barrels) was blown up by order of Sir John Moore, that it might not fall into the hands of the enemy, and such an explosion I never witnessed before; the sound was tremendous, and the volume of smoke, thick and black, that ascended was a wonderfully fine sight. Lutyens, Harding, and I were sitting in the chimney-corner in our cantonment near Corunna, when the magazine was blown up; the soot fell all about us, and we were ignorant of the cause of this terrible report, until we ran out of the house to see what was the matter, when we saw an immense column of black smoke rising from the ground; we then knew what had taken place.

A day or two before the Battle of Corunna I witnessed a very different sight, and a very painful one too, such as I hope never to see again; there being no ships provided for the embarkation of horses, an order was given out for them to be destroyed, and it was a cruel sight to witness the destruction of our fine English horses; many of them were brought to the edge of the rock overhanging the sea, some shot, and others stabbed, and then thrown down; of course very many of them reached the bottom alive, and there lay on the sands, poor things, where there were men placed to despatch them, frequently with a hammer; occasionally I saw a poor animal clinging to a rock previous to reaching the bottom. I could bear the scene but a short time and then went away; I never witnessed anything more horrible and painful, it was almost heart-breaking.

Many of the horses belonged to the Cavalry and Artillery, and many officers' horses belonging to the Reserve were amongst the

60

number. The nice little black pony, which I bought from the lady at Elvas, was one of the poor animals destroyed; he belonged to Colonel Ross, to whom I sold him previous to our retreating, for none but Staff and Field-Officers were allowed to have horses, forage being so scarce; besides it would have discouraged our men to see all the officers mounted. It was a sad end for my little black, and I was very sorry when I heard of his fate.

Colonel Ross had a beautiful chestnut Arab, which was also one of the horses shot on this day; he had brought him from Egypt to Malta in 1801, and had been offered a hundred and fifty guineas for him in England, by, I believe. Lord C——; he was a very handsome charger and much admired.

The day the Reserve arrived at their cantonments near Corunna, I was ordered to remain with my company, detached from my regiment; Sir John Moore happened to pass through the village where we were, as he was riding round the outposts; seeing us he rode up to me and asked who I was; I told him I was captain of the *20th* Light Company; he immediately said it was a mistake our being left there, and ordered me to join my regiment, as he wished that the Reserve should have a little respite, having recently gone through so much during the retreat. I thought that Sir John Moore made his enquiries and gave his orders to me in such a mild gentlemanly way; I was quite struck with his engaging manners, and so were my two subalterns; and I am sure the men of my company seemed, all of them, to be equally pleased with him. Alas! a few days afterwards he was no more, "*sic fortuna belli.*"

At Corunna, one fine winter afternoon, the 16th of January, 1809, when we were all making ourselves as comfortable as circumstances would admit, by changing our linen, and the men cleaning themselves, their arms and accoutrements, (I mean the Reserve, for the troops of the other divisions had had opportunities before), a sudden firing was heard, both cannon and musketry, which made a great stir amongst us, and we all equipped ourselves as speedily as possible, and in less than half-an-hour we were under arms, and marching towards the point attacked, for the French had commenced an action and were advancing towards our lines. The French force amounted to 20,000, and that of the English to 14,500 men.

On our way there, Lutyens and I had a narrow escape; a cannon shot pitched close in our front, but the ground being soft it buried itself, and only saluted us by throwing up the dirt round about us. It was a severe action and lasted until dark (from 3 p.m. to 6 p.m.); many of our regiments suffered severely, and we unfortunately lost our excellent and brave commander, Sir John Moore; but the French were completely beaten in all points, and as soon as the action was over, it was decided that the troops should be embarked. The first to embark were the Reserve, an arrangement made a day or two before, by Sir John Moore, in consequence of the fatigue they underwent during the whole of the retreat.

A few hours after we had lost our brave commander the Reserve embarked; it was about two o'clock in the morning, and a cold morning too in the month of January; happy enough we were to get on board ship, and, although it was very dark, most of us reached the ships allotted to us. You may well suppose that we were rather hungry after our previous exertions, and fortunately for my party we found on board a fine large camp-kettle of soup, the making of which I myself had superintended, in the garden of the house where we were quartered when the Battle of Corunna commenced; little expecting, at that time, to have eaten it on board ship. This soup was of course cold and a perfect jelly; it had boiled for hours, and a man of my company, being left behind sick, had taken charge of it and carried it on board with him. The soup was soon demolished, and we then turned into our berths, and had the luxury to sleep without our clothes, and once more to get into a bed, the first time for some weeks. In the morning, soon after daylight, we sailed out of the harbour, glad enough to get out of the country.

Previous to our sailing from Corunna we left some of our troops on shore to assist the Spaniards in covering the embarkation of the remainder of our army; and I believe before night closed all were on board and off for "Old England," rejoiced to get away after our disastrous retreat.

It was well known that many Spaniards, who were enemies to their own country, frequently gave the French information which was detrimental to our cause. What commander could therefore stay in a country like this? If Sir John Moore had received greater reinforcements, and at an early period, it was thought that he might have kept his ground, and the result would have been far different to what it was; but Sir John was unsupported in all ways. I always looked upon the death of Sir John Moore as a great national loss; the army too regretted greatly the death of their gallant commander, for he was a fine, noble, brave fellow, and most courteous in his manners, whenever he gave any orders to the officers or men.

He was likewise a very clever man and a good general, but he never had a force sufficient to cope with the enemy; and the Spaniards behaved in such a dastardly manner, running away to their homes,—particularly after we had commenced our retreat,—instead of harassing the enemy to the utmost of their power; so that, being left to ourselves, our force was nothing, in point of numbers, when compared to that of the French; we were therefore obliged to get out of the country.

Poor Sir John Moore was buried at Corunna. I visited his tomb in 1812 when on our way to join Lord Wellington. The tomb was quite plain, without any inscription, having a cannon sunk in the ground at each corner; some time afterwards the Spaniards put an inscription on it. I believe that the Spaniards erected the tomb, as our army were all off the day after the action, and had no time to make the necessary arrangements.

CHAPTER 11

The Walcheren Expedition

In a few days we arrived at Falmouth. Of course, naturally enough, some of us were glad to get on shore, and, as soon as we reached it, numbers of the inhabitants flocked round us to enquire about the. fate of Sir John Moore's army, as it had been reported in England that we were all taken prisoners. Such appeared to have been the general rumour, as no despatches had reached home for some time, and they were at a loss to know what had become of us. We soon told them all the news, and of the death of our brave commander, which the people appeared truly sorry to hear.

Our stay at Falmouth was very short. We were ordered to Spithead, disembarked soon after, and marched to Colchester barracks, where we were quartered until about the month of August, 1809, when we were ordered on the expedition to Walcheren. We marched to Dover Castle, and during the week we were marching there it rained almost every day, which was rather unfavourable for a regiment going to such an aguish country as Holland. We remained in the Castle about a week, and then embarked on board an old 44-gun ship (I forget the name), commanded by Captain Dodd, which took the whole of the regiment. Our embarkation took place at Deal, and we sailed from the Downs the next morning. The Downs at this time appeared like an immense forest; it was supposed that there were not less than from 800 to 1000 vessels lying at anchor.

We sailed with a large fleet and arrived off the Dutch coast on the following morning; our voyage, being short, was (to me) very agreeable; we had a great many on board, at least 900, including the ship's crew. Although our passage was only twenty-four hours, we were sixteen days on board ship from the time we embarked until we disembarked. The old *20th* soon disembarked at South Beveland. We were likewise quartered in other islands in the Scheldt, North Beveland, and Wolversdyke, and most unhealthy they proved to the troops. We were in these islands a few weeks, and both officers and men suffered dreadfully from fever and ague. Captain South and our surgeon. Dr. Arnott, were both very seriously ill.

The day we disembarked we marched to a place called Heinrich's Kindren, where I remained with the regiment one day, and was then ordered, with two companies, to the village of Borssele, to take possession of two batteries (about a mile off) on the dykes near the sea; and which the French had evacuated a few days before, destroying the ammunition and spiking the guns.

In this village another officer and I were billeted at a private house, where we met with every civility; we lived entirely with the family, for they would not allow us to cook a single thing. A division of our army was at Walcheren, and the French were in Flushing, 7000 strong. Constant firing took place between our gun-boats and their batteries, and as we were only three miles from Flushing across the water, we could see all that was going on. The village we occupied was in a very pretty little island (South Beveland), abounding in vegetables, particularly potatoes, which were excellent; you hardly saw a piece of ground uncultivated; as for the towns they were remarkably clean and the houses very neat.

During the whole time we were in these islands the regiment never fired a shot in action, nor hardly ever saw a Frenchman, except one day just before we left Wolversdyke, when some spies came into the island and were approaching our quarters in a covered cart, driven by a Dutchman; but they were discovered by Colonel Ross, who was ever on the alert; he immediately pursued them with a few of the Light Company, who let fly some shots at them, but they got off, and we could find no trace of them.

After remaining in these pestilential islands a few weeks, and having almost the whole of our men on the sick-list, we quitted the country. As a proof of the unhealthiness of these islands I need only mention, that the farmhouse, at South Beveland, where two companies were quartered under my command,—for I was then major,—was thus situated:—a field with a broad ditch of water round it, with about three feet of mud at the bottom, over which was a plank to cross, and the farmhouses were not far from the ditch; the consequence was that fever and ague daily—indeed I might almost say hourly—made their appearance amongst us. I myself have seen whole families ill with this dreadful complaint, shivering over their fires. If therefore the inhabitants of these islands were subject to this distressing malady, what could we expect?

Those officers who continued in health amused themselves with country sports, shooting and fishing. We used to kill wild ducks, and also partridges, upon Louis Buonaparte's estate, he being nominally King of Holland.

One day, while out with my gun, I met with an unfortunate accident. When leaping over a ditch with a pole I strained my back; it was very sudden, for as soon as I had leaped over, my feet dropped under me as if I had been shot, and I had the greatest difficulty in getting back to my quarters; and the lumbago to which I have ever since been subject, I mainly attribute to this accident. I was laid up for several weeks in these unhealthy quarters, but I had no attack of ague until I returned to England.

Previous to our embarking in the Scheldt we had but few men on parade for they were constantly dropping down in the ranks, consequently our numbers were daily diminishing, and glad indeed we were to get away. The last place we were in was Wolversdyke, a small island about four or five miles in length and three or four in breadth, from which we embarked. When we marched from our cantonments we left a few men under the command of Captain Murray[1] to watch the movements of the enemy, who were separated from us only a few hundred yards by a branch of the Scheldt, they being in North Beveland, where they were collecting boats to transport their men across to our side.

The orders Captain Murray received were not to conceal his men, but to have a sentry or two in the church tower, and, after giving us half an hour's start, he was to put his men into carriages which were

---

1. Afterwards Major Murray. He retired in 1818, and died shortly after at his native place, Jedburgh, in Scotland; we had passed nineteen happy years together in the old *20th.*

waiting for them, and to join us with all expedition. By the time he reached us with his men we had not far to march to where the *St. Fiorenzo* Frigate was at anchor to receive us; and no doubt, before we were all on board, the French had taken possession of our old quarters, which we had just left; and quite welcome they were to them, for we were very glad to quit such an unhealthy country, where we had encountered so much sickness.

The frigate in which we embarked was commanded by Captain Matson, who was most kind and attentive to us. We sailed one morning at six o'clock and reached Harwich about six the same evening. Just before we got under weigh we met with an accident which might have been serious, for while getting up our anchor the capstan gave way and came clean off by the board. The greater part of the men at the bars were our soldiers, and not a man of them was hurt. Captain Matson paid them a high compliment for their sailor-like management; our men had very often been on board ship, which made them rather handy and useful when their services were required.

After disembarking at Harwich we marched to our old quarters in Colchester Barracks, in the month of November I think, having been away nearly three months; we had about 600 men sick, and before we left England the old *20th* had 900 effective men. On our arrival at Colchester Barracks many were enquiring, "Where is the regiment?" And well they might, for having such a number of men sick, and many on duty with the baggage, etc., we did not march more than 200 men into the barrack yard, a miserable remnant of our former numbers. It was the most sickening and heart-rending campaign on which I had ever served; it was a melancholy sight to see our regiment march into the barracks, when we reflected that hundreds who had left them three months before in good health, were now seriously ill; many other regiments were similarly circumstanced.

The Walcheren Expedition, for the time it lasted, was more fatal to the troops than anything ever experienced in the West Indies for a similar period, as allowed by those who had served in those islands; and the misery which we suffered, from ague and fever, was far more distressing than the privations and hardships which we endured in Sir John Moore's retreat. I came home from the latter campaign in perfect health, although I had always marched at the head of my Light Company; but soon after my return from the Walcheren expedition I was seized with fever and ague, continuing ill for many months; and I did not join my regiment until the autumn of 1810, at Mallow.

After we returned from Holland we lost two officers by sickness,— Captain Robinson and Ensign Mills,—and a great number of men. The *20th* remained at Colchester until the summer of 1810, at which time they embarked at Harwich and sailed for Cork; from thence they went to Kinsale and afterwards to Mallow, where they were quartered until the spring of 1812. From Mallow they went to Fermoy barracks, stayed there during the summer, and then marched to Middleton in the same county.

CHAPTER 12

Portugal

At the time we arrived at Middleton we were under orders to proceed to Spain. The regiment remained but a few weeks in Middleton barracks before marching to Cove, where we embarked for Corunna early in October. I was on board the *Dover* frigate (Captain Drury). We had a long and tedious passage, being nearly a month on our way; the passage might have been quicker, but we got too far down in the Bay of Biscay; however, we had nothing to do but to obey the directions of the Commodore (Captain Horton), and our voyage was, consequently tediously long and irksome.

One evening, in most beautiful weather, I recollect we were tacking about close in to land, Under the Pyrenees. Some of these rocky mountains were excessively lofty and cragged, and the sun shining upon them gave them a most picturesque and splendid appearance. I never saw before, nor since, such a magnificent scene. Some of the rocks rose up into rugged peaks, somewhat similar to cathedral turrets, only of a more gigantic description; in short I cannot describe their grandeur. Often have I thought of them, for they made a great impression upon me at the time. It was a particularly fine bright evening, and, as we sailed along close under these stupendous mountains, it was a beautiful sight to see the gleams of the setting sun lighting up their lofty rugged summits with a golden hue. I little thought at the time that I should so soon be marching over the Pyrenees, though not exactly over the mountains now in view.

We landed at Corunna, but remained on shore only one day, when we proceeded to Lisbon. We were to have marched through the country to join Lord Wellington's army, but, as I suppose that it was considered a hazardous experiment for so small a force as ours to make the attempt, we were ordered to resume our voyage to Lisbon. We had but a short time, not more than twenty-four hours, to stretch our legs on shore; and we were very sorry to go on board again, as we should have preferred a march through the country. We were also disappointed at our stay here being so short, as we should have much liked to have gone over the ground where the Battle of Corunna was fought in January, 1809. We visited, however, the tomb of our brave commander, Sir John Moore; but not at all expecting that we were going to re-embark the day after we landed, we did not make such good use of our time as we otherwise should have done, for our orders were very sudden and unexpected. Such are some of the pleasures of a military life!

We had a very long passage to Lisbon also, for sailing under convoy makes the voyage frequently double the time; if our frigate had been left to itself to make its own way, no doubt we should have reached our destination (the Tagus) in half the time.

Previous to our landing at Lisbon, an unpleasant dispute took place between the captain of the frigate and the major in command of the troops (on board), all of my regiment. Our disembarkation was not a very pleasant one, being attended with great risk, for the boat in which the major and I landed—a man-of-war's launch—was laden nearly gunwale down, and the lieutenant, who had charge of her, was perfectly aware of our critical situation, and reported it to the captain of the frigate, who was on board the launch, and he immediately said that he would take charge of the boat himself, and he came on shore with us; we had about three miles to go, and, fortunately for us, it was pretty calm; for if we had happened to encounter one of those violent and sudden squalls incidental to that climate, it might have been attended with serious consequences; everything that belonged to us was ordered to be taken out of the frigate and put into the launch, except two horses, which belonged to the major and myself.

Our two horses were upon deck the whole time from the Cove of Cork to Lisbon—about seven or eight weeks—still they were landed in pretty good condition, although we were short of food for them, our hay and corn being nearly expended. The corn did run out, and we were obliged to give them peas occasionally. They had tarpaulins erected over them, and they were slung upon the deck near the main-mast, where they remained during the whole voyage, one on each side. As the horses never could lay down, we of course naturally felt anxious about them, and we were very happy to get them ashore, which was accomplished in safety.[1]

We had also with us a great deal of ammunition, all our baggage, besides officers, soldiers, women, etc.; in short it was touch-and-go with us, but we providentially reached the land in safety. While we were sailing towards the shore we were almost all silent, hardly a word was spoken, except occasionally an order from the captain about the sails, no explanation at this time having taken place between the two commanders with regard to their quarrel, but as soon as we landed high words passed; the consequence was a challenge was sent by the captain of the frigate to the officer in command of the troops, and I had the uncomfortable post (at his particular request) to attend him as his friend; and being satisfied that his conduct had been correct I could not well refuse, and happy I was that nothing serious took place after exchanging shots. I witnessed the whole of this unpleasant affair, but the less that is said about it the better; such occurrences as these are painful to think of.

We remained in Lisbon about a month. Near Lisbon there was a very fine aqueduct, the centre arch of which was supposed to be sufficiently lofty and wide enough to admit a first-rate man-of-war through it, with all sail set. This aqueduct was across a valley and supplied Lisbon with water.

We left Lisbon on the 15th December, 1812, and marched into the country to a place called St. Joan de Pesquira, which we reached on the 13th of January, 1813, after a march of twenty-nine days. Pesquira was situated on the river Douro. Our route to this place was first of all to Sacavem, thence to Lajuia, Pombal, Coimbra, and Visea. At this time we were appointed to the Fusilier Brigade, commanded by General Pakenham, and in General Cole's division. The weather was very wet now, though very mild, like May in England.

We were stationed at Pesquira during the winter of 1812, and until

---

1. I valued my horse very much, having bought him young (three years old). At this time he was five years old, and I rode him until he was seven; I then (in 1814) sold him for ninety guineas to Major-General Robert Ross, when I left Spain. Although he had been twice wounded in one action—the action of 25th July, 1813, in the Pyrenees—he was nevertheless perfectly sound.

the campaign opened in May, 1813; our quarters there were miserably cold, for the Portuguese had no idea of a comfortable fireplace, and frequently there was not a glazed window in the house; the consequence was, when we wanted light we were obliged to open a shutter instead of a window, so that we admitted cold as well as light, it was a miserable town, hardly a decent looking house in the whole place, except the one where the general (Lowry Cole) was quartered. We were glad to commence campaigning after passing the winter in such wretched comfortless quarters. I have sometimes put oiled paper, as a substitute for glass, in the windows of my quarters, that I might enjoy light without being taxed with the cold; no such comforts anywhere, after all, as in "Old England."

After we left Pesquira we were frequently encamped previous to the Battle of Vittoria, which took place the 21st June, 1813. Some time before the action took place I was sent to a town called Meda, at which time my regiment was at Almendra, about twelve miles off, I was sent to Meda to take charge of the hospital there, where there was a great number of sick, belonging chiefly to regiments that had been in the country two or three years.

Meda was situated in an open rocky plain, hardly a tree to be seen, except in the gardens of private houses; the house in which I had my billet was the best one in the place; my *padrone* being the head man there I had therefore good quarters, and being the commandant at Meda I had the advantage of a snug berth.

There was an excellent garden to the house, and the fruit trees were still in blossom when I left it. There was one very large tree—a cherry tree, I think—which had a most beautiful appearance, like one entire blossom, something resembling a large cauliflower, so round and white; it was quite a picture, and the contrast of the almond and other trees, added much to its beauty and to that of the garden.

The nightingales were very numerous here and sang delightfully, even at midnight, and the stillness of the place added much to the effect. The notes of these birds were not so soft as those in England, but much louder, and early in the morning they were sometimes very disturbing. One thing which was a great luxury in my quarters at Meda was a fireplace, which was rarely to be met with in that country; but it appeared that some British officers had occupied these apartments previous to my being there, and the *padrone* (I mean the master of the house) had allowed them to make fire-places and to build chimneys; as there are men of all trades in regiments masons were soon set to work, and the gentleman of the house and his family were so much pleased with the improvement, that they had fireplaces put in several rooms, so that the house was far superior to any in Meda; it had a miserable appearance to see the families in other houses sitting round a pan of charcoal, with their cloaks over their shoulders, half starved with the cold.

I had very little communication with the family, not speaking their language, and they did not seem much inclined to seek my acquaintance; but as there were a few officers of different regiments quartered here, we had a mess and a little society amongst ourselves, so that during the short time I was at Meda I had amusement and occupation, and the time passed pleasantly enough.

I remained at Meda a few weeks, and then the hospital was broken up, and I rejoined my regiment at Almendra, happy to get back to the old *20th*, It is a distressing sight to witness the removal of the sick of a military hospital on service, particularly in a convoy where there is such a want of comfortable conveyance as was now experienced. It was a sad scene to see the poor creatures, who should have been in their beds, some in open carts, others sitting on mules or asses, or walking; but such are the scenes in time of war witnessed by military men, and, painful as they must be, they cannot be avoided but must be endured.

At Almendra, as at Meda, nightingales abounded and were very noisy early in the morning, for the room in which a few of us slept had the roof so open in some places. that the sound came through the tiles, which were also so laid that, although we could see the light between them, still the rain never came in, and the weather at this time (May) being very hot. we suffered no inconvenience from the air admitted. The nightingales here were so tame that I have both seen and heard them singing in the middle of the day in the trees—close to our house—under which the soldiers were cooking their dinners, and they were not at all disturbed by the smoke of the fires or the talking of the men, but continued to sing cheerfully and merrily.

After I had joined my regiment at Almendra our stay there was but short, as about this time the regiments were breaking up from their cantonments, and were about to open the campaign.

CHAPTER 13

Spain & Vittoria

Shortly before leaving Almendra we (the 4th Division) were reviewed by Sir Thomas Graham. We left Almendra about the middle of May (1812), and marched thence into Spain; our route lay through Zanora, Toro, and Palencia. Toro I had been in with Sir John Moore's Army in 1809. Palencia was a very fine large town with a most beautiful cathedral; I regretted much that we did not halt there to see the lions, but Lord Wellington seemed determined to push the enemy. On the 11th June we were encamped near Sardine in Spain, having been on the march twenty-five days, all the time in close pursuit of the French army, without being able to come up with them. We were, at this time, only six leagues (two days' march) from Burgos, but did not know whether our column was to besiege that place, or whether we were to cross the Ebro to Vittoria, for Lord Wellington of course kept his plans very secret.

Including Spaniards and Portuguese our army amounted to about 110,000 men, of which 40,000 were British. Lord Wellington frequently passed us on the march, and reviewed our division once. We used to march every morning between three and four o'clock, generally reaching our camping ground about 10 a.m. The roads were remarkably good, resembling our own in England and there were no hills. Salisbury Plain was a joke to what we met with in the country through which we passed, for the eye could not reach the extent of the plains over which we marched; they abounded in game, and at one of our encampments I am sure that I do not exaggerate when I say, that our division killed a hundred hares.

Until the Battle of Vittoria (21st June, 1813) we were sometimes on the march, at other times encamped, occasionally in bivouac or in quarters, but more frequently on the move, expecting every now and then to meet the enemy; at last came the Battle of Vittoria. I recollect being on horseback that day (21st June, 1813) from about five in the morning until nine at night, with the exception of occasionally dismounting for a short time; and, as we had neither forage for our horses nor food for ourselves, until the battle was over, we were glad when the enemy retreated, for it was a hard day s work, and I think we all earned our day's pay. It was a brilliant action, lasting from 9 a.m. until dark; but the old *20th* had only a few men put *hors de combat* today—three killed and three wounded. It is impossible to be always in the thick of it, and we had plenty to do and to contend with in many other hard-fought engagements.

The Brigade, in which my regiment was, consisted of the 7th Fusiliers, *20th*, and 23rd Fusiliers, a pretty little brigade, and was in the 4th Division, commanded by Lieut.-General Lowry Cole; our division was not called the fighting division, but the supporters; the 3rd Division, under General Picton, were named the fighting division; each division had some quizzical name given to it.

I recollect on this day seeing a Portuguese regiment (the 21st, I think,) in our division, marching as steadily in line, with their colours flying, and advancing towards the enemy as if they had been moving on a parade; they were officered by British, and the men were generally looked upon as very good soldiers, having behaved very bravely in many actions.

During this battle the cannon shot, etc., were flying about in all directions, but my horse was very steady, though many passed over us as we advanced. Joseph Buonaparte (King Joseph, as he was called,) was nearly taken prisoner; he had to quit his carriage and mount a horse, and was within an ace of falling into our hands; some of our dragoons came up on one side of his carriage, while he escaped out of the other, and the road was so choked with guns, wagons, and the debris of a fight and rout, that our men could not get round in time to capture His Majesty. I saw the carriage captured; Lord Wellington got all his plate.

Our entrance into Vittoria was so unexpected by the French, that it was said the dessert was upon King Joseph's table; however, his Majesty had a very different kind of dessert; for instead of grapes he had grape-shot.

The enemy were driven in all directions, and lost 151 pieces of cannon, all their baggage, ammunition, military chest containing a good deal of money—twelve million dollars—and a great number of carriages, horses, mules, etc. The road was blocked up with a long line of carriages, cannon, wagons, carts, horses, and mules, without any drivers, extending an immense way, all deserted by the enemy. Among them were several private carriages; one contained the Countess of Gazin, the wife of a French General, with her servants and some other ladies; but the Duke of Wellington very politely sent one of his *aides-de-camp* to escort them into their own lines.

Our division marched past all these spoils on the road, still continuing to pursue the enemy until it was dark; we were not allowed to take anything as we moved along, it was look at all things, but touch nothing, much to our disappointment of course; but such a restriction was perfectly right, so as to prevent disorder and confusion. It just shews the discipline of our men, who could pass such treasure and yet refrain from plundering.

In the afternoon of this day a circumstance took place which rather displeased our general, but we thought it excusable; the men had not had anything to eat all day, and had been on their legs marching for many hours; we happened to come alongside a field of beans, the men immediately broke the ranks, dashed into the field, and came out each of them loaded with beans pulled up by the roots, which they devoured voraciously. Frequently during our campaigning our men had to eat boiled wheat; sometimes they imprudently ate it unboiled, which was very unwholesome, causing illness from indigestion; in short, at times we were glad to get anything we could. Those who have never served on a campaign cannot be aware of the privations to be endured when soldiers are on active service; it requires rude health and strength to withstand the numerous hardships to which they are subjected.

We pursued the enemy until darkness overtook us, for the French were thoroughly beaten and completely routed; they were driven some way beyond Vittoria; when night came on we bivouacked. We did not get any forage for our horses or food for ourselves until after nine at night, and then it was all chance; for the men went from our bivouac to search for forage in the dark, so that they hardly knew which way to steer. However, by good luck, they found a field of standing corn, some of which they cut and brought to our animals, and they devoured it with great voracity.

A few other officers with myself did not fare badly after all, for we procured a cold fowl and something else, part of the plunder, I believe, taken in the action; for among what fell into our hands there appeared to be a little of almost everything. The only things I got were a goat and a saddle cloth; the goat soon came to a melancholy end; I had it fastened to the stirrup of my horse which was picketed not far from me, but unfortunately my horse was alarmed at something during the night,—perhaps at the goat, at least I supposed that was the reason,—lashed out, and kicked the animal so severely, that I had her carried upon one of my mules for a day or two, in hopes she would have recovered, but the poor thing died, and I blamed myself for having placed her in that dangerous situation, attached to the stirrup. It was a very handsome goat, and would have supplied me with plenty of milk, a great luxury in these times to take with our tea after a fatiguing march.

Unfortunately the country where the action took place was so mountainous that our cavalry could not act. If we could only have engaged the enemy on a plain they would have been cut to pieces, for we had at least 6000 cavalry in the field that day. At one time during the action the Life Guards were close to my regiment; they looked nobly.

The next morning our bivouac presented a curious scene; men belonging to the Brigade disposing of various spoils which had been taken, and many soldiers wives were decked out in ladies handsome and valuable dresses, plundered from the French wagons, in which there was women's as well as men's baggage; some of the men got a great deal of money; the scene was a perfect rag fair, such a variety of good and bad articles. I recollect, during the Battle of Vittoria, seeing Colonel The Hon. H. Cadogan, of the 71st Regiment, lying dangerously wounded, attended by two or three of his corps; he was, I believe, an excellent officer, and much respected in his regiment; he died of his wounds, greatly lamented.

CHAPTER 14

Roncesvalles

The French were still almost daily pursued, but they retreated some way before they again made any stand against us, and our brigade had not much to do, in the fighting way, until July; we had a good deal of marching and bivouacking, but no serious engagement, only now and then a little skirmishing. On the 11th of this month we had been forty-seven days on the march, including a general action, but I was none the worse for our fatigues. We had marched at least 500 miles, pursuing the enemy many days after the battle of Vittoria. We had terribly cold and wet weather at this time, which was very trying. One day when encamped at Aybar, near the Pyrenees, we had such rain that it beat through our tents, and some officers had their baggage floating about.

Sometimes during our pursuit a gun was taken, and now and then a battery, but my regiment had not any more fighting of consequence until the 25th July (1813); on this day the action was sudden and unexpected, for between our brigade and the enemy was a high hill, called the heights of Roncesvalles, and we were not exactly aware of the force, which the French had behind it The point where this engagement commenced was on the top of the heights,—which were in front of our brigade,—up which the left wing of the *20th* Regiment was advancing; with this little force was Major-General Ross, who commanded the brigade; Lieut.-Colonel Wauchope commanding the *20th*, and I (the junior major), were likewise with the wing, besides Captain George Tovey and some other officers, whose names I cannot exactly recollect. We marched up the hill, leaving the other wing of the regiment in a wood at the foot of it.

Brevet-Major Rose of the *20th* commanded the Light Companies of the brigade, and advanced in front of the left wing, acting as rifle-men; but the superior force of the enemy soon drove them in. In rear of all was the remainder of the brigade, the 7th and 23rd Fusiliers; just as some companies who were in advance, under the command of Captain Tovey, reached the top of the hill, the French came up on the other side and met them, and many were bayoneted on both sides; however, finding the enemy were so strong,—having thousands to our hundreds,—we were all obliged to retreat down the hill in double quick. I had my horse wounded, but fortunately escaped untouched, though I had some narrow escapes that day.[1]

In this action, called the combat of Roncesvalles, we suffered a great deal, particularly in officers. We had the misfortune to lose our Adjutant, Lieut. R. Buist; he was the first officer who fell, being killed early in the action; he was a fine active fellow, although in weight at least eighteen or twenty stone, and was very attentive to his duties as Adjutant. Lieut.-Colonel Wallace was severely wounded, and shortly afterwards died; I had served in the *20th* with him, poor fellow, from 1795 until 1813; he was a brave officer. Captains Bent and Cham-pagnè were also wounded, besides some others whose names I cannot call to memory now; but altogether one killed and eight wounded; we also had a good many men killed and wounded.

My horse was wounded in the neck on the off side, and below the ribs on the near side; a third bullet went through the flaps of my saddle, and a fourth lodged in my boat-cloak, which was rolled up in front of my saddle; but providentially I escaped without a scratch. The ball in my horse's neck was extracted by a medical officer, I think of the 23rd Fusiliers; the other ball was not found, it was supposed to have fallen out.

On the morning of this engagement we were stationed in a village, and were called up early to march to the scene of action, it having been discovered that the enemy were on the move towards us in great force; so away we went, not having many miles to go, all ready for a brush with them. Poor Buist, the adjutant, came into my room to call me up, and to apprise me of the order to march; little did I think at that time, that in a few hours he would be no more; alas! how uncer-

---

1. *Vide* Appendix C.

tain is life.[2]

After the action we retired into the wood and remained there the whole day, the French occupying the opposite hill, from which we had been driven by such superior numbers in the morning. We were firing at each other all day, and were almost every moment expecting them to come down and endeavour to drive us out of the wood. They had so large a force it was astonishing that they allowed us to remain in our position; but probably they thought we had a large reinforcement at hand, which was not the case; if, therefore, they had advanced we must, it was supposed, have given way, and it might have turned out an unfortunate day for us; for General Cole, with part of the 4th Division, was two miles at least from us, on our right; and if we had been driven from our position his force would, in all probability, have been cut off.

I was sent by General Ross to General Cole during the action, to ask him for reinforcements, but his answer was, "Tell General Ross he *must* keep his post, for I cannot render him any assistance"; as far as I can recollect these were his words. Previous to my being sent with the message my horse had been wounded, and not having another I could not ride quite so fast as I otherwise should; however, I returned with the answer pretty expeditiously, for at this time my horse had been wounded but once.

As I was returning with the general's answer I fell in with, on the road, our poor Scotch piper; he was badly wounded in the thigh, but unfortunately I had no means of assisting him, and he must have been taken prisoner, and no doubt died of his wounds, as the regiment never heard of him afterwards; he was a harmless, inoffensive fellow, and we regretted his loss.

General Cole was, as I have shewn, particularly anxious that we should keep our ground, which we did until night came on, when we were obliged to retreat and to take up a new position, for we were completely overpowered by numbers. When we left the wood that night, being unable to take away those who were severely wounded and totally incapable of being moved, we were obliged to leave them behind, lying under the trees, poor fellows, wrapped up in their blankets. It was melancholy to have to resort to this. There was one man

2. *Vide* Appendix D.

of ours, I recollect, about whom our surgeon, my good friend Dr. Arnott, was very anxious, being convinced that he could not live from the serious wound he had received; but just before we marched off Arnott came up to me and said that the poor fellow had just expired; it appeared a great satisfaction to him, and so it was to me; he was an old soldier well known to us, and he was in a melancholy state to leave behind.

CHAPTER 15

Sauroren

After quitting the wood we took up a new position either on the 26th or 27th; it was a very commanding one on a lofty hill, opposite to which the French were posted upon another hill more elevated than ours, a deep ravine only separating us; the two armies, in a direct line, being little more than a mile from each other. At night it was curious to see the fires along their line, and ours must have been equally conspicuous to them; they had a large force, upwards of 30,000 men, and Soult commanded them.

It appeared to be their aim to relieve Pamplona, which was but a short distance from either of the armies. On the morning of the 28th July (1813) we were on the look-out expecting an attack, and at last it took place, but the enemy were beaten at all points, and could not relieve the garrison of Pamplona, which place surrendered to our army some little time afterwards.

During this action the French met with very great loss, for they came down the ravine in dense columns, and, as we had the command of the heights on both sides of the ravine between their army and Pamplona, we fired into their columns and did great execution. Some of their force attacked our position, but they met with determined opposition, and the old *20th* was one amongst the number who charged them on that day. It was a hard fight while it lasted, the French losing more than 5,000 men. They must have been dreadfully disappointed, not being able to throw supplies into the garrison of Pamplona, which was in sight of their army; and the garrison must also have witnessed the action, and felt equally annoyed at seeing their army driven back.

In this battle[1] our regiment was divided into two wings, Lieut.-Colonel A. Wauchope commanded one wing, and I commanded the other, being now second in command, in consequence of our senior Major (Brevet Lieut.-Colonel Wallace) having been dangerously wounded on the 25th July. We lined part of the side of the hill and kept up a heavy fire upon the enemy as they advanced. The French on that day did not make the attack very early, it being a wet morning. If they had attacked us earlier one of our divisions would have been absent, I think it was the 5th Division, and Lord Wellington was very anxious for them to join us, having observed that the French troops were on the move. We could see the enemy very distinctly from our position, and (with my glass) I observed Soult several times that morning mounted on a mule. These mules are the safest animals to ride in these mountainous countries, which were particularly slippery after much rain, and the rain, it was supposed, was the reason why Soult did not make his attack at an earlier hour.

I recollect being very near Lord Wellington that morning, and I could occasionally hear his Lordship's remarks. He was anxiously looking out all the time, with his telescope, for the absent division, his glass being directed towards the point where his Lordship was every minute expecting to see them advancing. At last one of his staff reported they were coming; Lord Wellington then said, "Now they may attack us as soon as they like." The absence of this division would have been a great diminution to our force, for they were about 5,000 men. The French were actually beginning to advance before the 5th Division hove in sight; this was enough to make any commander fidgety; this division came up on the opposite side of the ravine to that on which we were posted, so that their opportune arrival gave us the command of both the hills, between which the French advanced with Pamplona in their front and in sight of them. It was an anxious time for all.

I do not exactly recollect what loss we had on this day, but Captain Edward Jackson[2] of the *20th* was wounded, and a very fine young man, Lieut. John Hankey Bainbrigge, lost an arm.[3] We also had several

1. Called the first battle of Sauroren.
2. Afterwards major in the regiment, and in 1838 an unattached Lieut.-Colonel He died 1841.
3. Now (1878) General Bainbrigge: he was for many years Fort-Major of Guernsey.

men killed and wounded. At this time we were not very strong in officers having had about 15 officers and 240 men put *hors-de-combat* in the last two actions. Our army suffered nothing, however, when compared with the losses of the enemy.[4]

After the French had failed in their attack they retired to their former position; the next day they retreated and we pursued them. Whilst they were on the move in the morning they were somewhat astonished by our firing some Shrapnel shells amongst them, as we had got a gun up on the heights early that morning. It was drawn up, I believe, by the sailors, who are famous fellows at anything of this kind. I saw the French scampering away when the first shot was fired, not expecting we could get a gun up such a height. It carried completely across the ravine, and I heard that one of the shells did great execution, killing and wounding about twenty-four men, as was reported to have been said by a French prisoner afterwards taken; and this was not at all improbable, as it pitched into a column, which it completely dispersed.

This day (29th July) we were encamped on the mountains near Pamplona, and the French were opposite to us, about three or four leagues off.

What with fighting and marching I was nearly exhausted with fatigue, for since my horse had been wounded I had been obliged to walk, and we marched, one time, two nights together; however as my horse's wounds healed rapidly I was soon able to mount him again.

After the enemy retreated we continued to follow them and were occasionally skirmishing; on the 1st August we were engaged with the French, as also on the 2nd,[5] on which day the old *20th* suffered a good deal, having had one officer (Ensign Wrixon, quite a youth) killed, and our commanding-officer (Lieut.-Colonel Wauchope) dangerously wounded; I then took command of the old regiment in the field.[6]

---

4. Lord Wellington in writing of this action called it "fair *bludgeon work*."
5. On the heights of Echalar.
6. Lieut.-Colonel Wauchope was desperately wounded and died a few weeks afterwards, poor fellow, when I was appointed Lieut.-Colonel of the *20th*; I had then been only seven or eight weeks Brevet Lieut.-Colonel, so rapid was my promotion in this campaign. Poor Wauchope was buried at Passages, where he died. A few days before his death I sat by his bedside and wrote a letter to his father in Scotland, which he dictated, asking his father to meet him at Portsmouth, as he was daily expecting to embark at Passages for that place; but, alas! (continued next page.)

This campaign was certainly a very dismal one, for although I had great promotion, still it was in a melancholy way, by loss of old friends. At the time I took the command of the regiment, in the action of the 2nd of August, I was only second Major, Brevet Lieut.-Colonel Wallace being then ill of his wounds received at Roncesvalles, and of which he shortly afterwards died.

After the action of the 2nd of August my regiment was pretty quiet, as far as not being *actually engaged* with the enemy constitutes quietness; for although we were frequently advancing and taking up new positions, it did not fall to our lot to be again engaged for some little time; however, as we had had a pretty fair share of honour and glory lately, it was therefore not to be expected that we could always be fighting. Sometimes we were so posted that our brigade could see what was going on among some of the other divisions, although in reality we had not much to do with it; but the country being so mountainous, a part of our army might be engaged, and we be mere spectators.

On the 21st August (1813), being the anniversary of the Battle of Vimiera, in Portugal,—which took place in 1808, and was the first action fought in that country by Lord Wellington (then Sir Arthur Wellesley),—he invited all the officers of the 4th Division, who were actually in the battle, to dine with him. We sat down about fifty, six or eight of which belonged to my old regiment. We had a splendid dinner, plenty of champagne and claret, and an excellent dessert consisting of peaches, grapes, etc. His Lordship was very affable; and I recollect that, after dinner, he said, looking round the table, how happy he was to see so many of his old friends who were with him in that action. The toast of the 21 St August, 1808, was afterwards drunk with great glee.

At this time we were encamped near a place called Lezaca, in Spain. About the latter end August I paid a visit to the works before St. Sebastian, which was about six leagues from our camp, along a terribly bad road. St. Sebastian was situated on the top of a high hill close

---

it was not to be. At the time of his death, Lieut. Wm. Chafin Grove of the *20th* was with him. There was always somebody of his regiment in attendance; many of us went to stay with him, but Grove was always at his quarters, and was very kind and attentive. He had the best medical advice, as surgeons of the army constantly visited him.

to the sea, and about a mile from Passages, where our poor Colonel (Wauchope) was then lying badly wounded, and where there was a harbour with a good number of transports in it at the time. The place appeared very strong, and it was reported that our batteries were to open on it the 28th of this month.

We were now anxiously looking for the publication, in the English newspapers, of Lord Wellington's Despatches respecting the recent actions, and heard that he had not forgotten to mention my regiment for their conduct on the 25th July, at Roncesvalles; we also understood that his Lordship had mentioned very handsomely the conduct of our division (the 4th) for their gallantry on the 28th July, when Soult attacked us.[7] We also read in the *Moniteur* that Soult said that on the 25th July *he totally annihilated my regiment*.[8] We could have told him a very different story, for we could have next day brought into the field more than *four hundred survivors* of that fight.

We were encamped near Lezaca for several weeks, a much longer time than at any other place we had been in since the campaign opened; still we were always obliged to be on the alert, ready to move at a moment's notice.

7. Appendix E.
8. Appendix F.

CHAPTER 16

St. Jean de Luz

On the 31st August (1813) an engagement took place between the French and Spaniards, when the latter behaved *nobly*. We were not engaged on that day, being in reserve, and for several hours close to Lord Wellington, who seemed the *coolest* man under fire that could possibly be. Our position was on a height called the Crown Mountain, whence we were spectators during the whole time, with our arms piled, and perfectly at ease. We distinctly saw the Spaniards and French engaged, the former being in a strong position on a height, above a town called Irun, at the foot of which ran the river Bidassoa, which here divided Spain from France. We saw the French cross the river, ascend the hill, and attack the Spaniards, but they were driven back; still they repeated their attack several times, sometimes forcing, for awhile, the Spaniards, and at other times being worsted.

The Spaniards sent to Lord Wellington for a reinforcement, but his Lordship had observed the gallant manner in which they were behaving themselves, and refused support, saying they should have the honour of the victory entirely to themselves, as his Lordship was satisfied that they would, in the end, be conquerors; which they were, and drove the French again across the river. The Spaniards behaved particularly well that day, and dashed at the French in noble style. The French lost a great number in recrossing the Bidassoa; we were very glad to see the Spaniards retain their position.

The mountain being very lofty where the action was fought, I could see a long way into France. I saw a very fine town, called St. Jean de Luz, and many others still much further off; we likewise had a fine view of the sea, being not more than a league from it.

At the time that the action took place our troops were also storming St. Sebastian, an anxious time for Lord Wellington. I saw him take out his watch several times, for he had (I believe) given orders for the place to be stormed at noon, and, hearing heavy firing there after that hour, he was evidently very anxious to learn the result of it. I remember an *aide-de-camp* riding up about 3 p.m. and saying, "My Lord, St. Sebastian has fallen"; they then talked together, and his Lordship seemed much affected at hearing that many of his old friends had been killed.

At the siege of St. Sebastian I lost my most intimate friend in the Regiment, Major Rose; we had been together nearly eighteen years, and I felt his loss most deeply. He was a fine high-spirited, brave young Scotchman, the handsomest officer in the *20th*, and of an excellent temper; he was a great favourite among all ranks in the regiment, and much regretted by everybody, and by no one more than myself, as our attachment to each other was like brothers. At the time he was killed he was in command of about 200 men,—volunteers from the various regiments of the 4th Division,—who led the storming-party at St. Sebastian, and where, poor fellow, he fell.

When he marched his detachment from the 4th Division a day or two before the place was stormed, I went part of the way with him, walking alongside his horse; he was talking to me a good deal about the duty on which he was going, well-knowing what an arduous one it was, and he seemed to have a presentiment that he should never return; for when I took leave of him, and wished him every success, and said "God speed you, my dear fellow," he said "God bless you, I shall never see you again." I then walked back to the camp to my regiment, which I then commanded, and I must confess that I felt much out of spirits at what my dear friend Rose had said at parting; and a few days after we heard of the sad event of his death, so that his words had proved too true, "I shall never see you again"; and much hurt we all were at the melancholy tidings.

We suffered severely both in officers and men during this summer campaign, having had five officers killed, nineteen wounded, and 271 men killed and wounded; I was the only Field-Officer in the old *20th* who escaped unhurt.

My regiment was not seriously engaged with the enemy for some time, and about the middle of September (1813) we were encamped near the Bridge of Yanzi. At this time we found our tents very cold and damp at night, for the rain frequently came down in torrents, and beat through them; but there was nothing to do but to grin and bear it.

I recollect one day (I forget the date), when the French attacked a body of Portuguese troops, some little distance from our position, I was observing, to an officer of my own regiment, that the Portuguese were driving the enemy; Lord Wellington, who was standing very near at the time, turned round and remarked, "What is that you said. Sir?" I answered that the Portuguese were driving the French, his Lordship then said, "I saw that." Lord Wellington appeared to be always on the lookout and let nothing escape him. At another time, I recollect, the French took up a position with a large force exactly opposite the *left* of our line which was likewise in position. Lord Wellington, with his Staff, was reconnoitring and was heard to say that afternoon "not a man of them will be there in the morning."

His Lordship's prediction was verified, as the enemy moved during the night for the purpose of attacking the *right* of our line, no doubt thinking we should wait expecting to be attacked, on our *left*, by the force opposite to us on the previous evening; but the great commander was up to their *ruse*, and moved his force that same night as soon as it was dark, so that, in the morning, the enemy seeing us again opposite to them were completely foiled in their plans, and thoroughly outwitted by the great captain, the noble and gallant Wellington.

In the middle of October we lay encamped on the heights above Sara, France, in sight of Bayonne which was situated in a most delightful fertile plain; we were longing to leave our position in almost inaccessible mountains, which we found very cold and wet at this advanced season of the year, the rain sometimes coming down in torrents. We still continued to have frequent skirmishes with the enemy, but our losses were slight.

One day I went to St. Sebastian, and of all the ruinous places I ever visited this surpassed anything I had seen before; it seemed to have been a large town, and at this time there was hardly a house standing; even the churches were very much injured by the shot and shells, and the castle itself, although situated on a high rock above the town, was a complete ruin. I visited the breaches where the troops entered, and where many a fine fellow fell; a melancholy sight it was.

On the night of the 16th October we had a dreadful storm, and the wind blew so violently, that it was with difficulty we could keep our tents standing: the rain came down in such torrents that it beat through my tent, and almost everything in it was drenched.

My horse had now quite recovered from his wounds, but looked thin on account of the bad weather to which he was exposed, for he was never under shelter; and, besides, we had to send about *twenty miles* over the mountains for forage, and as each horse held to fetch his own supply, the poor animals underwent greater hardships than we did.

We were in daily expectation of an attack by the enemy, and kept on the alert day and night, for the order was not to take off our clothes.

CHAPTER 17

The Nive

Our Division (the 4th) was quartered, for about a fortnight, at a village called Ascain, whence we marched at daylight on the morning of the 8th of December and encamped. The next morning the enemy attacked the centre of our line, and our division went in support, but the enemy were repulsed, and we were not engaged.[1] On the 10th December the enemy attacked our *left*, and the day after the *right* of our line, but they were *completely* beaten in *every* attack they made, and retired with great loss. We had a good deal of marching, for the 4th Division were at every point where the troops were engaged, being the supporters, and therefore having to move wherever our assistance was required; consequently we had more marching than any other division. For eight days we were without our baggage, and for two or three nights without tents, exposed to rain and sometimes frost.

On the evening of the 11th, just after dark, when the action was over for that day, and the French were retiring from their position, we were all agreeably surprised by the arrival of three German regiments, who had deserted and come over to our brigade—the Fusilier Brigade. They were very fine looking fellows, and their officers came over with them; they were without their baggage, which had been left at Bayonne; their bands were also there; however they had plenty of bugles, and took good care to blow them as soon as they were safe in our lines. It was about ten o'clock when they arrived, and we gave them a very good supper, for they got three bullocks and plenty of rum and biscuit; they were then marched to St, Jean de Luz; there were about 1300 of them, and their grenadiers were the finest men I ever saw.

1. This was on the occasion of the passage of the Nive.

Some of them told me that when they went into action they used to *bite off the balls* and merely to fire *blank* cartridges at us, shewing how averse they were to the French, and how much they respected our nation. They said that there was another infantry regiment, and likewise one of dragoons, ready to follow their comrades' example; but it was feared that Soult would now send them to the rear, and not give them the opportunity of deserting.

We were all getting very tired of the campaign, which seemed to weary the most zealous. The advanced season of the year rendered the constant exposure to cold and wet weather most trying. We used often to say, when in cantonments near Arrauntz on Christmas-Day, 1813, how differently our friends at home were employed. They were enjoying sumptuous fare compared with us, who were glad to get our food in any shape and at any time, being always on the alert, and having to breakfast and dine whenever an opportunity offered. My regiment being at this time so scattered about at different houses, we could not eat our Christmas dinner together. Some of the houses were nearly a mile apart, and the roads were dreadfully muddy; and as for riding to each other's quarters, not having any thing for our animals to eat, we were obliged to let them graze all day to keep them from starving; my poor favourite horse continued to look very thin, much more so than *his master*, who was very well, although occasionally threatened with ague.

The part of the army we were with at this time was between the Nive and the Nivelle, but Sir R. Hill had a large force over the Nive, with his right resting on the Adour, and he had a good many cavalry with him. We were about six or seven miles from Bayonne, not knowing whether we were to besiege that place or not.

I had plenty to do now, being in command of the regiment; it was very weak from the severe losses we had sustained, but we hoped to get a good number of volunteers from the Militia.

The surrounding country was very beautiful and there was excellent shooting in the neighbourhood, but we had no dogs; and besides this the weather was so stormy that there was little pleasure in going out of doors, and I was glad to sit by a fireside, a great novelty to us, I wanted to visit Pamplona, but it was too far off; being obliged to be always on the alert, we could not go far from our cantonments.

At eight o'clock, on the night of the 3rd January, 1814, we went away very suddenly from Arrauntz. After a few hours marching we fortunately got housed for the night, for we had left without baggage or tents. We made off again at 4 a.m. on the 4th, marched all day, and encamped at night. The next day we did the same, and on the morning of the 6th we started again to drive the enemy over the river Arran. About three o'clock in the afternoon of that day we came up with them; they were posted on the heights at a short distance from the river; the 3rd Division was on our right and part of the 2nd Division on our left, ours (the 4th Division) being in the centre; the enemy were attacked in all three points, and in about an hour and a half they were driven across with very little loss on either side; our brigade were not engaged, but we saw the whole business. I was standing near Lord Wellington during almost the whole of the time; he was looking very earnestly through his glass, and seemed much pleased with the conduct of his troops.

After the affair was over we bivouacked for the night,—our tents being in the rear,—and a very cold night we had of it; fortunately it did not rain, and the next morning we marched into cantonments at a place called Usteritz, where we remained some weeks; in fact the weather was so very wet that the roads became impassable, and neither army could move.

One day, while here, some of our men in charge of several mules, belonging to officers of different regiments, were out foraging, when they were all captured by the enemy; some of the mules were mine, but I did not regret the loss of the mules, so much as I did that of the men, for they were all old soldiers and very good men, a great loss to the regiment.

The house in which I lived at Usteritz was very pleasantly situated, close to the river Nive. It was a water-mill, and the inhabitants were very poor people, but very civil. The only objection I had to it was the clack of the mill, as well as the noise of the water-fall close under my window, but I got accustomed to these sounds. All kinds of provisions here were very dear: three shillings a pound for butter and cheese; half-a-crown a pound for sugar; tea sometimes as much as ten and twenty shillings a pound; meat two shillings a pound; a dollar for a quire of paper, and everything else in proportion. We were also very badly off for money, having at this time *six months pay due to us*. We were about a league from Bayonne, which seemed a fine town.

CHAPTER 18

War's End and Ireland

My regiment now had not been seriously engaged with the enemy, for some time, and as the campaign appeared to have come to a close,—for the Dutch at this time had risen to shake off their yoke—and it was supposed that the French would have been obliged to quit the lower Pyrenees, I therefore took the opportunity of obtaining leave of absence in the month of February (1814) and proceeded to England on urgent private affairs. However, it so happened that the campaign was unexpectedly resumed, and two actions were afterwards fought,—the battle of Orthes, 27th April, and the battle of Toulouse, 10th April, (1814).

The *20th*, at the battle of Orthes, was commanded by Major Bent, who, poor fellow, unfortunately fell that day, as also did Captain St. Aurin; several officers were wounded and many men killed and wounded in this action: at the battle of Toulouse the regiment had a few men killed and wounded.

Major Bent had been wounded 25th July, 1813, and also at the landing in Egypt, 8th March, 1801, when in the 92nd Regiment; he was a very good officer, and had been many years in the *20th*; I much regretted his loss, as we were great friends.

The battle of Toulouse ought never to have been fought, as the French commander well knew that peace had been made, but never apprized Lord Wellington of it. It was therefore a useless sacrifice of men on that day, entirely owing to the conduct of the French General.

Brevet-Major Russell succeeded to the command of the *20th* Regiment at Orthes, and brought them to Ireland after they quitted

France, where they embarked at Bordeaux.[1]

I joined the *20th* at Waterford the 19th of August, 1814,—having been absent a few months and being now married,—and resumed the command of the regiment. During part of the time that the *20th* was at Waterford I was staying at Tramore, a small watering-place; there were fine sands here, so wide at low water and so extensive, that the races were held on them in the summer. The distance from Waterford being not more than seven or eight miles, I could constantly ride in to visit my regiment,

We had a good deal of pleasant society whilst in Waterford, and found the inhabitants very kind and attentive to the regiment. A young man joined us here, son of the mayor of the place, named Henry Sargent; a fine young lad, who, I poor fellow, died afterwards in India, a lieutenant in the 44th Regiment.

We remained at Waterford until the autumn of 1815, at which time we marched to Templemore Barracks, County Tipperary, One advantage of being quartered at Templemore was the regiment being concentrated, which was seldom the case in any quarter in Ireland, there being such numerous detachments, a state of things which is very injurious to the discipline of a corps; however, we had the good fortune to be kept together during the whole of our stay here, which was for about six months, and our barracks were very commodious. It was a very retired place; only a few families round about us, Sir John Garden, Bart., Dowager Lady Monck, Captain Webb, and Mr. Garden, of Barnane, who were all very attentive to us, and to many of the other officers.

We had sometimes very unpleasant duties to perform in Ireland, parties going out to seize stills, to prevent illicit distillation of whiskey. These parties were generally commanded by subaltern officers. Sometimes, also, parties were ordered out to search for arms, sometimes to assist driving in cattle for rent, and occasionally to search for people who had been guilty of attending unlawful meetings at night, etc.

I once went out with the regiment to search for arms, with Sir

---

1. Brevet-Major Russell afterwards retired on half-pay, and is now (1838) gone to New South Wales with his large family. He was in the *20th* Regiment with me for nineteen years, and was for some time my subaltern in the Light Company; we were therefore very old friends, and I trust and hope he may succeed in his undertaking in New South Wales.

John Garden, a magistrate; after traversing many miles of country, visiting numerous cabins, and searching them, we could not find a single stand of arms; If there were any they were so concealed that we could not discover them. It was supposed they were secreted underground.

In Ireland, unfortunately for the military, soldiers were often employed in duties which, in England, were invariably performed by the civil power, and which frequently were very unpleasant for them.

From Templemore we went to Boyle, county of Roscommon, where we continued from the spring of 1816, to the summer of 1818. In this quarter we were much detached, the regiment being in *nineteen* different places, among them Cashcarrigan, Ballinamore, Killeshandra in county Cavan, Elphin, Drumsna, and various others. Part of the regiment was also at Sligo, under Major South, so that at head quarters (Boyle) I had only about 300 men, and but few officers under my immediate command. Our barrack was one large house, which had formerly belonged to the Kingston family, but had been purchased by the Government: it held most of the men, and several officers. In this house my son Charles[2] was born, on the 5th of April, 1818; soldiers were both above and below us, the officers' quarters being the centre range, so that I may say he was born to be a soldier.

I had very comfortable rooms in this house, and I liked Boyle as a quarter very well. The river Boyle ran close by the barrack wall: in this river I amused myself fly fishing, and there were two or three fine lakes within a short distance, one, Lough Kay, which belonged to Lord Lorton; and his lordship was kind enough to allow the officers to fish in them, and he also lent them a boat. I myself have caught trout in Lough Kay six pounds weight, and some weighing nine pounds were also taken.

There were several families round about Boyle, who paid great attention to many of the officers; we visited Lord and Lady Lorton, and two families of the name of Elwood, one at Hollybrook, and the other at Ballymore, besides some others. Lord Lorton's place, Rockingham, was a magnificent seat, and his lordship was very kind to his tenants; many men were constantly employed on the estate, and Lord Lorton

---

2. He entered the army in 1840, served in the 2nd West India, 28th, and 32nd Regiments, and fell in action at Chinhut, during the Siege of Lucknow, June 30th, 1857, Captain 82nd Regiment.

resided very much at Rockingham.

In November, 1817, the unexpected death of H. R. H. The Princess Charlotte of Wales took place, and on the occasion of her interment, on the 18th of that month, the troops were directed to attend Divine Service.[3]

After continuing at Boyle until the summer of 1818, we were ordered to Dublin. At the time we marched to Dublin, the weather was so particularly sultry, that we used to start about two o'clock or never later than three in the morning, so as to have our marches over before the heat of the day commenced; and I found it a good plan, for our route was completed without much fatigue, and little or no sickness took place.

General Sir George Beckwith was commander of the forces in Ireland, and previous to our arrival in Dublin, I had heard he was a reserved stiff man, but I found him far otherwise; for when I had my first interview with the general, he very cordially shook me by the hand, and said he was very happy to see me and my regiment; that his father had been in the old *20th*; and during the time we were in Dublin we found the General a pleasant officer to serve under; he was likewise extremely hospitable and gave numerous entertainments, dinner-parties, etc., and was always particularly attentive to young officers. It only shews that characters sometimes, are, in reality, very different to what they are represented to be.

I remained with the regiment in Dublin until the autumn of 1818, when I obtained leave of absence, and came over to Cheltenham; and on the 18th December, 1818, I was gazetted out of the old *20th* Regiment,—having retired from the service by the sale of my commission,—and I was succeeded by Lieut.-Colonel Samuel South.

Lieut.-Colonel Steevens received a gold medal for the actions on the Pyrenees (July 28th to August 2nd, 1813); and also the silver war medal, with seven clasps, for Egypt, Maida, Vimiera, Corunna, Vittoria, Nivelle, Nive.

---

3. Appendix, G.

Appendix

A.

Extracts from Naval and Military Despatches, relative to the death of Major-General Robert Ross, who fell in the attack on Baltimore, September 12th, 1814:—

Rear-Admiral G. Cockburn, in a despatch to Vice-Admiral, The Hon. Sir Alexander Cochrane, dated H.M.S. Severn, in the Patapsco, September 15th, 1814, writes:—

It is with the most heartfelt sorrow I have to add, that in this short and desultory skirmish my gallant and highly valued friend, the Major-General, received a musket ball through his arm into his breast, which proved fatal to him on his way to the waterside for re-embarkation. Our country. Sir, has lost in him one of its best and bravest soldiers, and those who knew him, as I did, a friend most honoured and beloved; and I trust. Sir, I may be forgiven for considering it a sacred duty I owe to him to mention here, that whilst his wounds were binding up and we were placing him on the bearer which was to carry him off the field, he assured me that the wounds he had received in the performance of his duty to his country caused him not a pang; but he felt alone anxiety for a wife and family dearer to him than his life, whom in the event of the fatal termination he foresaw, he recommended to the protection and notice of His Majesty's Government and the country.

Colonel Brook, in a despatch dated H,M,S. Tonnant, Chesapeake, Sept 17th, 1814, writes:—

At this moment the gallant General received a wound which proved mortal He only survived to recommend a young and unprovided family. Thus fell, at an early age, one of the brightest ornaments of his profession; one who, whether at the head of a regiment, a brigade, or corps, had alike displayed the talents of command; who was not less beloved in his private than enthusiastically admired in his public character. If it were permitted to a soldier to lament those who fall in battle, we may in this instance claim that melancholy privilege.

From Vice-Admiral, The Hon. Sir Alexander Cochrane, Commander-in-Chief on the North American Station, to the Admiralty, dated H,M.S. Tonnant Chesapeake, Sept 17th, 1814:—

It is a tribute due to the memory of this gallant and respected officer to pause in my relation while I lament the loss that His Majesty's service and the Army, of which he was one of the brightest ornaments, have sustained by his death. The unanimity and the zeal which he manifested on every occasion, while I had the honour of serving with him, gave life and ease to the most arduous undertakings. Too heedless of his personal security when in the field, his devotion to the care and honour of his army has caused the termination of his valuable life.

B.

Route of the Reserve during the retreat of Sir John Moore, from Lisbon to Corunna, from notes by Lieut. W. W. Harding, of the Light Company *20th* Regiment:—

From the Camp at Becarinha to Aldea Galega;

,, Aldea Otdega to Cana	6	leagues.
To Montemore nuevo	4	,,
,, Vende de duc	7	,,
,, Aryolas	3	,,
,, Ustremos	2	,,
,, Alberoca	2	,,
,, Villa Vicosa	3	,,
,, Elvas	4	,,

(In Spain, Estremadura):-

To Campo Mayor	3	leagues.
,, Albuquerque	3	,,
,, Alcede	4	,,
,, Brosas	5	,,
,, Alcantara	5	,,

„	Sazza Mayor	5 „
„	Morilezza	5 „
„	Pezales	2½ „
„	Penio Pardas (Old Castile)	4 „
„	Guinelda „	2 „
„	Ciudad Rodrigo	3½ „
„	San Martini del Rio	5 „
„	Camillas di Abaxo	6½ „
„	Salamanca	3 „
„	Castilianos de Morisco	1 „
„	Cristofal di Cueste	½ „
„	Villa Excusor	6 „
„	Toro	4 „
„	Pedrosa del Rey	3 „
„	Tedra	2½ „
„	Villapando	4 „
„	Valdieras	5 „
„	Santierbo	6 „
„	Graghal di los campos	3 „
„	Mayorga	5 „
„	Fuente sa bucco	6 „
„	Benevente	2 „
„	Lavaniesa	7 „
„	Astorga	4 „
„	Combaros	2 „
„	Bembibre	6 „
„	Calcavelos	4 „
„	Villa Franca	6 „
„	Ferrareas	4 „
„	Nogales	6 „
„	Constantino	5 „
„	Lugo	5 „
„	Milarosa	1 „
„	Position	3 „
„	Position	3 „
„	Cordeda	6 „
„	Monilos	1 „

About 200 leagues = upwards of 800 miles.

C.

COMBAT OF RONCESVALLES.

(Copied from the United Services Journal for October, 1839.)

When Soult advanced into the Pyrenees, in 1813, with the intention of relieving Pampeluna, the Pass of Maia (I think it was) was held by the 4th Division. I forget whether my informant told me that an outpost had been surprised, but certain it is their Division was very much surprised one fine morning, to find the rugged ground in front of their encampment occupied by the enemy, who, without any ceremony, began blazing into their tents. Such things cannot occur without exciting especial wonder. The soldiers, half-dressed, began hurrying to arms, women and donkeys screaming, staff-officers madly galloping about ordering and expecting impossibilities.

The balls came flying thicker and faster from the enemy's rapidly increasing numbers, and the moment was fraught with disaster, when a gallant centurion, a choice spirit of the old 20th, at once came forth in character; his hundred bayonets quickly rallied at his call, and needing no order, with an enemy in front and disorder among his friends, he at once gave his own orders, "Fix bayonets, trail arms, double quick, forward"; in five minutes there was not a living Frenchman in the field; their skirmishers fled before him, and, in the sight of their whole Division, he with his single Company, with desperate and reckless charge, dashed into the head of a whole column of French infantry which had already gained the heights, overthrew them, and sent their whole mass rolling headlong and panic stricken into the valley below; it was one of the most brilliant feats of the war; it gave his division time to form and to commence that orderly and splendid retreat which terminated on the victorious field in front of Pampeluna.

George Tovey, where are you? for I have scarcely seen, scarcely exchanged two words with you, since these glorious days departed; twenty-six years have rolled over my head since this tale was told me by a brother officer of yours; the details may therefore be faulty, though substantially correct. I call upon you, as the hero of it, to inform the world whether you ever saw a British bayonet used; for if you brought your gallant band from that triumphant fray with bloodless weapons, you have been woefully belied.

Lieut.-Colonel George Tovey, I say, come forth! for if you do not, by my pen I swear that I will continue telling tales of the same kind against you, until I kindle such a flame in your cheek as may set fire to your scarlet coat, and make a hole in your half-pay, which it can but ill afford; for though the illustrious Wellington rewarded you, at the moment, with a Brevet-Majority, it was all that the miserable policy of the rulers of that day, at home, permitted him to bestow. Men of minor note, have since been exhibiting their pictures in panoramas and print-shop windows, while all that the public has ever seen or heard of you is, when some hungry hotel keeper at Cheltenham, or elsewhere, finds Lieut.-Colonel tacked to your name and sticks it in the newspaper as a lure for others, not knowing or caring who George Tovey is; this must no longer be, and again I say. Come forth, and for the honour of the bayonet answer for your charge!

You may not thank me for the call, but I know the public will, for drawing aside the curtain which has so long hung between them and you.

(Signed) J. Kincaid.

Reply to the above Letter, copied from the U. S. Journal for November, 1839.

THE CHARGE OF A COMPANY OF THE *20TH* REGIMENT AT RONCESVALLES.

Mr. Editor,—In the last number of your journal there is a letter from the gallant rifleman (Captain Kincaid), who, during the last French War, had so many opportunities of appreciating the value of a British soldier.

As there are one or two trifling inaccuracies, and I have been, besides, called upon by name to pronounce upon the authenticity of the bayonet encounter he has related, I shall do so as briefly as possible.

In the first place, the 4th Division, on the 25th July, 1813, did not occupy the Pass of Maya; they were between it and Roncesvalles.

Secondly, the Division had been expecting an attack that morning, and the *20th* Regiment were lying in column by their arms. It was daylight when a German Sergeant of the Brunswick Oel Corps, who had been out in front, came in haste to tell us that the enemy were close upon us, and that they had made the Spanish Picquet (who were posted to give us intelligence) prisoners, without firing a shot The left wing of the *20th* was moved instantly to form upon some strong ground in the direction they were coming, and, while doing so, the enemy's light troops opened so galling a fire, that Major-General Ross, who was on the spot, called out for a company to go in front; without waiting for orders, I pushed out with mine, and, *in close order and double quick* cleared away the skirmishers from a sort of plateau.

They did not wait for us, and, on reaching the opposite side, we came so suddenly on the head of the enemy's infantry column, who had just gained a footing on the summit of the hill, that the men of my company absolutely paused in astonishment, for we were *face to face* with them, and the French officer called to us *to disarm*; I repeated *bayonet away, bayonet away*, and rushing headlong amongst them, we fairly turned them back into the descent of the hill; and such was the panic and confusion occasioned among them by our sudden onset, that this small party, for such it was compared to the French column, had time to regain the Regiment, but my military readers may rest assured that it was required to be done in *double quick*. The enemy had many men killed, and the leading French officer fell close at my feet with two others, *all bayoneted*.

The Company, with which I was the only officer present on this occasion, did not amount to more than between seventy and eighty men, and we had eleven killed and fourteen wounded. I appeal to those of the 4th Division who witnessed this affair, whether I have arrogated to myself more than this handful of British soldiers are entitled to.

I have now responded to the call of the brave Rifleman, and followed up his random shot by a *bayonet thrust*; and as it is, in all probability, my last, either in the field or in print, I shall conclude by strongly advising our young soldiers to receive with caution the lucubrations of theorists, when opposed to the practical essays of the Duke of Wellington and other great Commanders, who have figured in history since the first invention of the bayonet

(Signed) George Tovey, Lieut.-Colonel.
Stanmore, 16th October, 1839.

N.B.—A powerful man of the name of Budworth, returned with only the *blood-soiled* socket of the bayonet on his piece; and he declared he had *killed away* until his bayonet broke; and I am confident, from the reckless and intrepid nature of the man, that he had done so.

D

Extracts from an Official Report and Napier's Peninsular War, respecting the "Combat of Roncesvalles"

General Cole to Lord Wellington, Heights in front of Pamplona, July 27th, 1813.

The enemy having in the course of the night turned those posts, were now perceived moving in very considerable force along the ridge, leading to the Puerto de Mendichurri, I therefore proceeded in that direction, and found that their advance had nearly reached the road leading from Roncesvalles Pass to Los Aldnides, from which it is separated by a small wooded valley. Owing to the difficulty of the communication the head of Major-General Ross's Brigade could not arrive there sooner. The Major-General, however, with great decision, attacked them with the Brunswick Company and three companies of the Twentieth, all he had time to form. These actually closed with the enemy, and bayoneted several in the ranks. They were, however, forced to yield to superior numbers, and to retire across the valley. The enemy attempted to follow them, but were repulsed with loss, the remainder of the Brigade having come up.

The 20th Regiment, under the command of Lieut.-Colonel Wauchope, were principally engaged on the 25th, and the conduct of the three companies, which, with the Brunswick Company, formed the advance, was particularly distinguished. Major-General Ross mentions particularly Captain Tovey of that regiment.

Extract from Colonel W. F. P. Napier's History of the Peninsular War vol. 6.

Before this message[1] could reach Cole, the head of Ross's column, composed of a wing of the 20th Regiment and a company of Brunswickers, was on the summit of the Lindouz, where, most of unexpectedly, it encountered Reille's advanced guard; the moment was critical, but Ross, an eager, hasty, soldier, called aloud to charge, and Captain Tovey of the Twentieth, running forward with his company, crossed a slight wooded hollow, and full against the front of the Sixth French Light Infantry dashed with the bayonet. Brave men fell by that weapon on both sides, bat numbers prevailing, these daring soldiers were pushed back

---

1. A message sent by General Campbell to General Cole apprising him of general Reille's force.

again by the French. Ross, however, gained his object, the remainder of the Brigade had come up and the Pass of Atalosti was secured, yet with a loss of 140 men of the Twentieth Regiment and forty-one of the Brunswickers,

E.

Extracts from Wellington's Despatch, dated San Estevan, 1st August, 1813, respecting the actions of the Pyrenees.

In the action which took place on this day (July 25th) the 20th Regiment distinguished themselves . . . . . .In the course of this contest (July 28) the gallant 4th Division, which had so frequently been distinguished in this Army, surpassed their former good conduct. Every regiment charged with the bayonet, and the 40th, 7th, 20th, and 23rd four different times. Their Officers set them the example, and Major-General Ross had two horses shot under him.

F

Extract from an Official Report from Marshal Soult to the Minister of War, after the combat at Roncesvalles, on the 25th July, 1813.

Linzoin, 26 Juillet, 1813.
Leurs pertes out également été considerables, soit à. l'attaque du Lindoux par le Général Reille ou le 20me Regiment a été presque detruit, à la suite d'une charge à la baionette, executée par un bataillon du 6me leger, soit à l'attaque d'Altobisca par le Général Clauzel.

G.

Western District Order.
Assistant Adjutant General's Office,
Athlone, 16th November, 1817.
Tuesday next, the 18th instant, being the day appointed for the interment of Her Royal Highness the Princess Charlotte of Wales and her Infant, the troops in the Western District will, on this most afflicting and solemn event, attend Divine Service; and the Officer Commanding at the different stations will be pleased to call upon the respective Garrison Chaplains to deliver a discourse suitable to the occasion.
The deep impression, which the untimely loss of the nation's future hope must have stamped upon every feeling mind, renders it unnecessary for Major-General Buller to attempt to expatiate upon its woes. He is fully aware in addressing those who have

gallantly shed their blood in support of the honour and dignity of the British Empire, that they have hearts to deplore the untimely loss of that exemplary Princess, who, (if Providence had permitted,) was one day destined to sway its sceptre.

By order of Major-General Buller,

(Signed)

J. P. Murray, Lieut.-Colonel, A. A. G.

The Officer Commanding
20th Regiment, Boyle.

LEONAUR

ALSO FROM LEONAUR
AVAILABLE IN SOFTCOVER OR HARDCOVER WITH DUST JACKET

JOURNALS OF ROBERT ROGERS OF THE RANGERS *by Robert Rogers*—The exploits of Rogers & the Rangers in his own words during 1755-1761 in the French & Indian War.

GALLOPING GUNS *by James Young*—The Experiences of an Officer of the Bengal Horse Artillery During the Second Maratha War 1804-1805.

GORDON *by Demetrius Charles Boulger*—The Career of Gordon of Khartoum.

THE BATTLE OF NEW ORLEANS *by Zachary F. Smith*—The final major engagement of the War of 1812.

THE TWO WARS OF MRS DUBERLY *by Frances Isabella Duberly*—An Intrepid Victorian Lady's Experience of the Crimea and Indian Mutiny.

WITH THE GUARDS' BRIGADE DURING THE BOER WAR *by Edward P. Lowry*—On Campaign from Bloemfontein to Koomati Poort and Back.

THE REBELLIOUS DUCHESS *by Paul F. S. Dermoncourt*—The Adventures of the Duchess of Berri and Her Attempt to Overthrow French Monarchy.

MEN OF THE MUTINY *by John Tulloch Nash & Henry Metcalfe*—Two Accounts of the Great Indian Mutiny of 1857: Fighting with the Bengal Yeomanry Cavalry & Private Metcalfe at Lucknow.

CAMPAIGN IN THE CRIMEA *by George Shuldham Peard*—The Recollections of an Officer of the 20th Regiment of Foot.

WITHIN SEBASTOPOL *by K. Hodasevich*—A Narrative of the Campaign in the Crimea, and of the Events of the Siege.

WITH THE CAVALRY TO AFGHANISTAN *by William Taylor*—The Experiences of a Trooper of H. M. 4th Light Dragoons During the First Afghan War.

THE CAWNPORE MAN *by Mowbray Thompson*—A First Hand Account of the Siege and Massacre During the Indian Mutiny By One of Four Survivors.

BRIGADE COMMANDER: AFGHANISTAN *by Henry Brooke*—The Journal of the Commander of the 2nd Infantry Brigade, Kandahar Field Force During the Second Afghan War.

BANCROFT OF THE BENGAL HORSE ARTILLERY *by N. W. Bancroft*—An Account of the First Sikh War 1845-1846.

LEONAUR

ALSO FROM LEONAUR
AVAILABLE IN SOFTCOVER OR HARDCOVER WITH DUST JACKET

THE 2ND MAORI WAR: 1860-1861 *by Robert Carey*—The Second Maori War, or First Taranaki War, one more bloody instalment of the conflicts between European settlers and the indigenous Maori people.

A JOURNAL OF THE SECOND SIKH WAR *by Daniel A. Sandford*—The Experiences of an Ensign of the 2nd Bengal European Regiment During the Campaign in the Punjab, India, 1848-49.

THE LIGHT INFANTRY OFFICER *by John H. Cooke*—The Experiences of an Officer of the 43rd Light Infantry in America During the War of 1812.

BUSHVELDT CARBINEERS *by George Witton*—The War Against the Boers in South Africa and the 'Breaker' Morant Incident.

LAKE'S CAMPAIGNS IN INDIA *by Hugh Pearse*—The Second Anglo Maratha War, 1803-1807.

BRITAIN IN AFGHANISTAN 1: THE FIRST AFGHAN WAR 1839-42 *by Archibald Forbes*—From invasion to destruction-a British military disaster.

BRITAIN IN AFGHANISTAN 2: THE SECOND AFGHAN WAR 1878-80 *by Archibald Forbes*—This is the history of the Second Afghan War-another episode of British military history typified by savagery, massacre, siege and battles.

UP AMONG THE PANDIES *by Vivian Dering Majendie*—Experiences of a British Officer on Campaign During the Indian Mutiny, 1857-1858.

MUTINY: 1857 *by James Humphries*—Authentic Voices from the Indian Mutiny-First Hand Accounts of Battles, Sieges and Personal Hardships.

BLOW THE BUGLE, DRAW THE SWORD *by W. H. G. Kingston*—The Wars, Campaigns, Regiments and Soldiers of the British & Indian Armies During the Victorian Era, 1839-1898.

WAR BEYOND THE DRAGON PAGODA *by Major J. J. Snodgrass*—A Personal Narrative of the First Anglo-Burmese War 1824 - 1826.

THE HERO OF ALIWAL *by James Humphries*—The Campaigns of Sir Harry Smith in India, 1843-1846, During the Gwalior War & the First Sikh War.

ALL FOR A SHILLING A DAY *by Donald F. Featherstone*—The story of H.M. 16th, the Queen's Lancers During the first Sikh War 1845-1846.

LEONAUR

ALSO FROM LEONAUR
AVAILABLE IN SOFTCOVER OR HARDCOVER WITH DUST JACKET

OFFICERS & GENTLEMEN by *Peter Hawker & William Graham*—Two Accounts of British Officers During the Peninsula War: Officer of Light Dragoons by Peter Hawker & Campaign in Portugal and Spain by William Graham .

THE WALCHEREN EXPEDITION by *Anonymous*—The Experiences of a British Officer of the 81st Regt. During the Campaign in the Low Countries of 1809.

LADIES OF WATERLOO by *Charlotte A. Eaton, Magdalene de Lancey & Juana Smith*—The Experiences of Three Women During the Campaign of 1815: Waterloo Days by Charlotte A. Eaton, A Week at Waterloo by Magdalene de Lancey & Juana's Story by Juana Smith.

JOURNAL OF AN OFFICER IN THE KING'S GERMAN LEGION by *John Frederick Hering*—Recollections of Campaigning During the Napoleonic Wars.

JOURNAL OF AN ARMY SURGEON IN THE PENINSULAR WAR by *Charles Boutflower*—The Recollections of a British Army Medical Man on Campaign During the Napoleonic Wars.

ON CAMPAIGN WITH MOORE AND WELLINGTON by *Anthony Hamilton*—The Experiences of a Soldier of the 43rd Regiment During the Peninsular War.

THE ROAD TO AUSTERLITZ by *R. G. Burton*—Napoleon's Campaign of 1805.

SOLDIERS OF NAPOLEON by *A. J. Doisy De Villargennes & Arthur Chuquet*—The Experiences of the Men of the French First Empire: Under the Eagles by A. J. Doisy De Villargennes & Voices of 1812 by Arthur Chuquet .

INVASION OF FRANCE, 1814 by *F. W. O. Maycock*—The Final Battles of the Napoleonic First Empire.

LEIPZIG—A CONFLICT OF TITANS by *Frederic Shoberl*—A Personal Experience of the 'Battle of the Nations' During the Napoleonic Wars, October 14th-19th, 1813.

SLASHERS by *Charles Cadell*—The Campaigns of the 28th Regiment of Foot During the Napoleonic Wars by a Serving Officer.

BATTLE IMPERIAL by *Charles William Vane*—The Campaigns in Germany & France for the Defeat of Napoleon 1813-1814.

SWIFT & BOLD by *Gibbes Rigaud*—The 60th Rifles During the Peninsula War.

LEONAUR

ALSO FROM LEONAUR
AVAILABLE IN SOFTCOVER OR HARDCOVER WITH DUST JACKET

OMPTEDA OF THE KING'S GERMAN LEGION *by Christian von Ompteda*—A Hanoverian Officer on Campaign Against Napoleon.

LIEUTENANT SIMMONS OF THE 95TH (RIFLES) *by George Simmons*—Recollections of the Peninsula, South of France & Waterloo Campaigns of the Napoleonic Wars.

A HORSEMAN FOR THE EMPEROR *by Jean Baptiste Gazzola*—A Cavalryman of Napoleon's Army on Campaign Throughout the Napoleonic Wars.

SERGEANT LAWRENCE *by William Lawrence*—With the 40th Regt. of Foot in South America, the Peninsular War & at Waterloo.

CAMPAIGNS WITH THE FIELD TRAIN *by Richard D. Henegan*—Experiences of a British Officer During the Peninsula and Waterloo Campaigns of the Napoleonic Wars.

CAVALRY SURGEON *by S. D. Broughton*—On Campaign Against Napoleon in the Peninsula & South of France During the Napoleonic Wars 1812-1814.

MEN OF THE RIFLES *by Thomas Knight, Henry Curling & Jonathan Leach*—The Reminiscences of Thomas Knight of the 95th (Rifles) by Thomas Knight, Henry Curling's Anecdotes by Henry Curling & The Field Services of the Rifle Brigade from its Formation to Waterloo by Jonathan Leach.

THE ULM CAMPAIGN 1805 *by F. N. Maude*—Napoleon and the Defeat of the Austrian Army During the 'War of the Third Coalition'.

SOLDIERING WITH THE 'DIVISION' *by Thomas Garrety*—The Military Experiences of an Infantryman of the 43rd Regiment During the Napoleonic Wars.

SERGEANT MORRIS OF THE 73RD FOOT *by Thomas Morris*—The Experiences of a British Infantryman During the Napoleonic Wars-Including Campaigns in Germany and at Waterloo.

A VOICE FROM WATERLOO *by Edward Cotton*—The Personal Experiences of a British Cavalryman Who Became a Battlefield Guide and Authority on the Campaign of 1815.

NAPOLEON AND HIS MARSHALS *by J. T. Headley*—The Men of the First Empire.

ALSO FROM LEONAUR

AVAILABLE IN SOFTCOVER OR HARDCOVER WITH DUST JACKET

ESCAPE FROM THE FRENCH *by Edward Boys*—A Young Royal Navy Midshipman's Adventures During the Napoleonic War.

THE VOYAGE OF H.M.S. PANDORA *by Edward Edwards R. N. & George Hamilton, edited by Basil Thomson*—In Pursuit of the Mutineers of the Bounty in the South Seas—1790-1791.

MEDUSA *by J. B. Henry Savigny and Alexander Correard and Charlotte-Adélaïde Dard* —Narrative of a Voyage to Senegal in 1816 & The Sufferings of the Picard Family After the Shipwreck of the Medusa.

THE SEA WAR OF 1812 VOLUME 1 *by A. T. Mahan*—A History of the Maritime Conflict.

THE SEA WAR OF 1812 VOLUME 2 *by A. T. Mahan*—A History of the Maritime Conflict.

WETHERELL OF H. M. S. HUSSAR *by John Wetherell*—The Recollections of an Ordinary Seaman of the Royal Navy During the Napoleonic Wars.

THE NAVAL BRIGADE IN NATAL *by C. R. N. Burne*—With the Guns of H. M. S. Terrible & H. M. S. Tartar during the Boer War 1899-1900.

THE VOYAGE OF H. M. S. BOUNTY *by William Bligh*—The True Story of an 18th Century Voyage of Exploration and Mutiny.

SHIPWRECK! *by William Gilly*—The Royal Navy's Disasters at Sea 1793-1849.

KING'S CUTTERS AND SMUGGLERS: 1700-1855 *by E. Keble Chatterton*—A unique period of maritime history-from the beginning of the eighteenth to the middle of the nineteenth century when British seamen risked all to smuggle valuable goods from wool to tea and spirits from and to the Continent.

CONFEDERATE BLOCKADE RUNNER *by John Wilkinson*—The Personal Recollections of an Officer of the Confederate Navy.

NAVAL BATTLES OF THE NAPOLEONIC WARS *by W. H. Fitchett*—Cape St. Vincent, the Nile, Cadiz, Copenhagen, Trafalgar & Others.

PRISONERS OF THE RED DESERT *by R. S. Gwatkin-Williams*—The Adventures of the Crew of the Tara During the First World War.

U-BOAT WAR 1914-1918 *by James B. Connolly/Karl von Schenk*—Two Contrasting Accounts from Both Sides of the Conflict at Sea During the Great War.

www.ingramcontent.com/pod-product-compliance
Lightning Source LLC
Chambersburg PA
CBHW031858090426
42741CB00005B/554